IMAGES OF IRISH NATURE

For Matthew, Rosie, Brad and Sarah
with all my love

IMAGES OF IRISH NATURE

by Mike Brown

With Foreword by Éamon de Buitléar

Published in 2006 by Mike Brown Photography
Clarke St, Clonakilty, Co. Cork, Ireland

Design by Ramona Stafford @ Mike Brown Photography

Pre press consultant Bart Van Put, Antwerp, Belgium

Text edited by Juanita Browne

Printed in Belgium by Daneels Graphic Group

All photographs copyright Mike Brown

All text copyright of the stated authors

Jacket illustration copyright Allan Cavanagh

Catalogue in publication. A CIP catalogue record for this
book is available from the British Library.

ISBN 0-9542863-1-6

Above. *Fallow deer on a misty morning*
Half Title page. *Common dolphins swim just under the
surface of a flat calm sea*
Page 2. *Fox cubs playing*
Title Page. *Lily pads on a bog pool*
Contents Page. *A Green-veined White butterfly*

Prints from this book may be purchased by contacting
Mike Brown Photography on +353 23 35782 or at
www.mikebrownphotography.com

CONTENTS

Acknowledgments

I cannot stress enough how lucky I am to have had the help of so many great people when it comes to doing this work. Without that help, whether it be physical help in setting up a hide or simply a snippet of information, I would not be as successful in getting my images. Behind the scenes there are helpers too. Those who have helped with the organising of this project or with my business in general. Others have simply encouraged me with their kind words and their love of my work. Without all these people I would not be able to follow this dream. To all those mentioned here I am eternally thankful. To anyone I have omitted through error, my deepest apologies. I hope this book will be a symbol of my gratitude to you all.

Thanks to my mum Annabel for all her support. To Kate and Pat, Mel and Ben and all my other family members for their support. Very special thanks to Terry and Carole and Tim and Sue for their help. To Jeremy, Annette, Bobby and Sally, to Pete and Fran and to Andy for their encouragement. To the wonderful Lynnie and Ian without whom so many of my pictures wouldn't exist! To Mike and June Fox for info and help. To Steve for being great. To Tony Nagle for great info. At BirdWatch Ireland; Oran O'Sullivan, Stephen Newton, Dave Sudabby and the fantastic Alex Copeland for making many things possible. To John, Brian and Kathryn in Banagher for their assistance. To Denis Mac, Barry and the staff at Denis MacSweeney photo shop for their help over the years. To Kieran and John at O'Leary's Camera World, ditto. NPWS staff John Griffin, Damien Clarke, Wesley Atkinson, Sr Enda Mullen, Michael O'Sullivan and Tim and Barry O'Donoghue. To Lorcan O'Toole in Donegal. To Derek Mooney at Mooney Goes Wild. To Declan and Saoirse and Bryan and Sara for loads of help and encouragement. To Caroline for her friendship. To Marian and Kemp Cooper for their hospitality and help. To Conor Kelleher for the late nights. To fellow photographers Eddie Dunne and Billy Clarke. To Mike McSweeney at Provision for his help. To Mark Coombes for his assistance.

Very special thanks to my lovely friend and great photographer Valerie O'Sullivan. A special thanks to Kevin Collins, for his immense knowledge, his enthusiasm and his hard work and to Sinéad, Cliona and Rory for their hospitality. To my parents in law, Leon and Josée without whom this project would not have been possible and for their special love and support. To Bart and family for his work and assistance and to Gerda and Kris and their families for their continued support. A special thanks to my Grandparents Dennis and Patricia who sadly won't see this work.

To the contributors to this book; Éamon, Juanita, Richard, Gordon, Damien, Michael and Pádraig, your contributions have given this book something special.

A very special thanks to Ramona, my right hand woman. For putting up with me changing my mind constantly and still doing a brilliant job designing and laying out this book. And for all her tireless work in the business.

To Ciara for organising me and to Máirín, Emer and Lucinda for all their help in the gallery.

Finally to my wonderful wife Rita and to our family; Matthew, Rosie, Brad and Sarah. My love for you all is endless.

Patrons

This book would not have been possible without the generous support of the organisations shown below.
To all those involved I offer my unending gratitude.

MARKET SHARE
IRELAND

CROSSING
THE LINE FILMS

Courtmacsherry
Hotel

O D M
ACCOUNTANTS

DILLON MULLINS
& COMPANY
SOLICITORS

• Niall O'Driscoll • Gearóid O'Driscoll • Dan Murphy
82 North Main St., Bandon, Co.Cork

AN ROINN COMHSHAOIL, OIDHREACHTA AGUS RIALTAIS ÁITIÚIL
DEPARTMENT OF THE ENVIRONMENT, HERITAGE
AND LOCAL GOVERNMENT

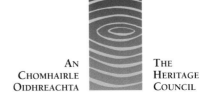

AN
CHOMHAIRLE
OIDHREACHTA

THE
HERITAGE
COUNCIL

This publication has received support from the Department
of the Environment, Heritage and Local Government

This publication has received support from the
Heritage Council

FOREWORD *by Éamon de Buitléar*

The peregrine falcon immediately took to the air and began screaming as soon as she noticed the two people winding their way up towards her nesting ledge on the high cliff. It was a warm June day with little wind and the alarmed falcon's repetitive warning calls echoed across the valley. The bird had reason to be scared; her three young downy white chicks were only five or six days old, and now they were seriously under threat as her arch enemy, man, moved ever closer to the nest.

During the previous winter my field assistant Frank had helped me to erect a number of hides in a remote high mountain area, where there were several traditional nesting sites used by peregrine falcons. The following spring our hopes were realized when a breeding pair of peregrines nested on a ledge directly opposite one of our hides.

As we worked our way up the slope towards the cliff-face to film the first nesting sequence, we intentionally made our approach quite obvious to the peregrines. This gave the falcon plenty of time to vacate the nest. If we were to suddenly appear out of nowhere, it would startle the bird and could cause the falcon to forsake the nest altogether. Photographing wildlife requires experience and a real understanding of the subject being filmed. Peregrine falcons are very sensitive to disturbance, especially during the early stages of the nesting season.

The location chosen for the hide was on a grassy ledge surrounded by clumps of heather, rough grasses and a lone rowan tree. In order to make the hide both invisible to humans and acceptable to the peregrines, we camouflaged it with a mixture of heather and bracken. It was quite difficult to see, even at a short distance and a mountain walker or climber passing by the cliff would hardly notice our secret hiding place. In order to create as little disturbance as possible, we erected the hide prior to the breeding season. There was even a dummy lens protruding from the viewing flap and pointing towards the nesting ledge. Peregrine falcons, in common with other birds of prey, have high visual sensitivity and it was important that the falcon and the teircel would both become used to having a large glass eye looking directly at them while they were in the vicinity of the eyrie.

As we climbed onto the ledge and reached the hide, the falcon was still soaring overhead. Her continuous harsh, scolding "rehk rehk rehk" cry had attracted her mate, the teircel, who was also joining in this somewhat unmusical chorus.

The normal procedure when filming birds of prey is to set up the equipment and have the cameraperson comfortably hidden inside the hide as quickly as possible. As soon as everything is in place, the assistant immediately leaves the location in full view of the birds.

People are often amused on being told that one of the reasons an assistant accompanies the cameraperson to the hide is that it is an old trick regularly used to confuse the birds! Once the assistant has moved off, the birds will come to the conclusion that both intruders have gone. Generally speaking, birds cannot count and peregrine falcons certainly do not have the ability to figure out how two people who were originally close to the eyrie, have now become a single individual heading off down the slope!

The peregrines will scout around for a while, and then gradually relax and provided they see no movement at the hide, should shortly return to the nest. When the pre-arranged time arrives for the photographer to leave the hide many hours later, the same procedure must be gone through in reverse.

I mention this particular filming episode purely as an example of what a photographer's experience might be when trying to capture a wildlife sequence on camera. Photographing animal behaviour requires good planning and rarely is it decided on the day to just go out and take a sequence of a particular mammal or bird. Capturing the final image usually involves quite an amount of research, long lonely hours of watching and waiting, and a fair amount of discomfort. Mike Brown could recount many such adventures in relation to his own collection of pictures.

Wildlife and photography go together and it is essential for a wildlife photographer to be familiar with the habits of the animals and to learn how best to approach them without causing unnecessary disturbance. This kind of knowledge only comes with experience and involves patiently spending time watching wild creatures in their natural habitats. The principles that apply to wildlife filmmaking are virtually the same as for stills photography. Most natural history photographers will tell you that they began first with an interest in wildlife and that the taking of pictures came later.

The experienced wildlife photographer will know that great care must be exercised at all times and particularly when photographing sensitive subjects, for instance ground-nesting birds such as hen harriers. A photographer's freshly made track leading to a nest can be an open invitation to an inquisitive fox to further explore the area. Carelessness in not taking steps to prevent the discovery of such a nest can result in the predator taking a complete clutch of eggs or a family of young chicks.

When photographing most forms of wildlife, it is important to avoid impacting negatively on the subject being filmed. Getting close to a female otter with very young cubs is one example of where matters could very easily go wrong for the photographer. An otter's first reaction to danger is to make a quick escape. A female otter will try to protect herself, rather than worrying at this point about the survival of her cubs. If she senses sudden danger at very close quarters, she will most likely panic and in the confusion might easily lose contact with her cubs. If she is too far away to hear their contact calls, the otter could decide to abandon them altogether. It need hardly be said that no photograph can justify creating that kind of situation!

Many of the creatures photographed for this book have had their actions frozen at just the right moment and are a good example of Mike's awareness of composition. Being able to apply a painter's eye to his photography is probably the result of his experience when as a young boy, he often watched his grandfather sketching in the countryside and painting in watercolours. It should be remembered however, that regardless of Mike's obvious artistic ability and sense of composition, it has taken a lot of personal effort on his part to reach such a standard of perfection.

Mike has been constantly presenting Ireland's wildlife in a most attractive way and his obvious knowledge of the countryside has enabled him to also include some interesting habitat photographs in this collection. Although Ireland may not have any particular species of mammal or bird that is not found somewhere else in the world, the various habitats and the manner in which some species have adapted to them are often in themselves interesting and attractive. One example is the Irish hare, which is a subspecies and similar in many ways to the mountain hare found in Scotland. The difference in the Irish hare is that it occurs not only in the mountains but also right down to coast. Another example is the Irish stoat, which is often associated with woodlands but in some areas along the shoreline it can be found searching for small fish in the vicinity of tidal rock pools.

In my young days there were few if any books in which Irish wildlife was explained and illustrated and there was certainly nothing even approaching a publication of this quality. My very first bird book was "*How to Recognize British Wild Birds*" by Eric Pochin and published in "The Young Naturalist" series. My first mammal book was "*A Beast Book for the Pocket*" by Edmund Sanders, which was also about British animals. Had it been my good fortune at that time to have a copy of Mike Brown's "*Images of Irish Nature*" in my possession, I would gladly have pored over its pages on a daily basis!

Mike's ability to produce a constant supply of excellent photographs not only sets a high standard for others to follow but his pictures also help to make people more aware of the beauty of Ireland's countryside and its wildlife.

Éamon de Buitléar   (July 2006)

INTRODUCTION

Photographing wildlife in Ireland, or anywhere in the world for that matter can be a difficult business. It is without doubt a succession of highs and lows and it can be both immensely rewarding and incredibly frustrating. Firstly, there just never seems to be enough time. Seasons come and go in the blink of an eye. The uncertainty of our weather doesn't help and the fact that animals don't always perform as you wish. These things can all make it even more infuriating. It seems that I often find myself chasing my own tail rather than that of my quarry. However, the joy of the highs - when an image turns out well, or even better than expected - always wins over the lows of perhaps spending eight hours in a hide and still not getting a picture.

After I had published my first book, "Ireland's Wildlife - A Photographic Essay" in 2002, I took a break from my wildlife photography. The project had been demanding and although I was thrilled with the reception it received from the public, I needed time to evaluate where I was going to go next with my wildlife photography. For about two years I stayed away from the wildlife work to concentrate on my commercial work and to pursue some other interests. During this time I decided to go ahead and work on a follow up to the first book. I set myself a target of two years to shoot a whole new set of images and this book is the result.

One of my aims was to include a lot of new subjects in this book. Whales and bats for instance were not included in "Ireland's Wildlife" and there is a vast number of birds, plants and insects in Ireland which also hadn't featured. So there was no shortage of subject matter. However, I also had other ambitions for this book. I wanted to experiment with movement and in particular, flight. Birds and bats fly as easily as we walk and when they take to the air they take on a whole new look. I wanted to show this great talent in the most beautiful way I could.

Some creatures do feature again in this book. We don't have a particularly large list of land mammals in Ireland so it was inevitable that some would appear again. Where this has happened I have tried to photograph them in very different ways than before. The emphasis this time, as I hope you will see, is more on the total image than on simply showing the perfect portrait. I also wanted to show some more abstract and simple views of nature such as dried seaweed on a shingle beach, snow in the Kerry mountains or the stunning granite pavements of the Burren at sunset. All these represent our nature perfectly in my mind. Finally, I wanted to ask some other people who are involved in Ireland's natural history, to become involved. Six writers have given us their thoughts, hopes, dreams and advice in essays, which are spread throughout this book. To me these essays conjure up further images of Irish nature and I hope you enjoy them as much as I did when I first read them.

While there may be a few lows in my work, there is nothing so wonderful as spending precious time in the Irish countryside. It is a great pleasure to enjoy its sights, sounds and smells. Or to spend time watching a wild creature as it goes about its business, unaware of your presence. I hope these new images bring those pleasures alive for you.

Mike Brown

Nature has many powerful forces; fire, wind and water come to mind but few are quite as exciting as an electrical storm. Thunder and lightning however, are much more common in other parts of the world, particularly the tropical regions. In Ireland they are few and far between and far more difficult to predict. This image was a grab shot at the tail-end of a short but spectacular storm in West Cork. Because it happened with little or no warning and just after dark, it was impossible for me to find a perfect location. However, the inclusion of the electricity pole was not an accident as I was happy to show both natural and man-made electricity in the same image.

Swallows fly at great speed and their agility is fantastic. This is one of about a dozen images I made of a pair that were nesting in a garden shed. Even though their entrance was narrower than their wingspan, they would fly in and out at full speed, opening their wings the moment they had passed through.

(left) When these swallows returned to their nest in a stable, they found it had been taken over by a pair of wrens. They built on a semi-detached nest and in time the female laid a clutch of eggs. With the female swallow incubating the eggs, the male became confused by the calls from the young wrens and would regularly come and feed them in between the visits of their parents.

At a distance the Green Hairstreak butterfly may be hard to notice.
When at rest on a plant it can look like a shiny leaf. These tiny
butterflies sparkle like emeralds at the start of summer.

When seen in close-up it becomes clear why the rare and beautiful Lady's-tresses Orchid is so named, with its swirling flowers wrapped around the stem like a dancers skirt in motion.

Harebells dance on the wind during the summer months and their soft colours brighten up many a pasture. I chose to isolate these two in this image as I loved the mirror-like composition.

In grasses as tall as its tiny frame, a Fallow deer fawn moves from the light into the shadow as it searches for its mother in the evening light.

A Hummingbird Hawkmoth is fascinating to watch as it flits rapidly from plant to plant hovering briefly over each one to feed. These immigrant moths arrive in the summer months from southern Europe and Africa.

(above left) *A ripe Wild Strawberry which I found along a ditch at the side of the road. After a photographing it I couldn't resist the temptation!*

(above right) *It is difficult to miss the bright colours of a Ladybird as it goes about its business.*

(left) *Primroses add a splash of colour to woodlands and ditches in the spring.*

Great Willowherb is common during the summer and I wanted to photograph it because of the beautiful colour of its flowers. It is however, difficult to make a striking image of this plant as it is quite untidy and straggly. I decided to photograph just the centre of a single flower head at three times life size, to isolate the colour and the delicate 4-lobed stigma.

After a long, hot day in the summer, I watched as the full moon began to rise over some forestry. The dust particles in the atmosphere made it glow with a yellow tint while it was still low in the sky.

Spring sunshine brings out the deep blue in the tiny flowers of the Germander Speedwell.

A Sika deer buck is surrounded by deep green and bright yellow as it forages amongst flag irises on a spring morning.

A Barn Owl leaves the stable where it roosts in the rafters during daylight hours, to go hunting for the night. The soft feathers of this bird ensure that it flies silently so as not to alert its unsuspecting prey.

Migrating to Ireland from southern Europe during the summer, the stunning Clouded Yellow butterfly lights up the meadows as it moves from plant to plant. When the sun is shining as it was here, it moves quickly and can be hard to keep up with. However, if a cloud obscures the sun it will often settle in the vegetation close to the ground like a golden leaf.

The first time I came upon a cluster of Fly Orchids I was very excited. The graphic shape and wonderful, deep colours, make it a perfect plant for photography.

Not all nature is beautiful. Magpies are disliked by most people as they will often prey on the young of garden birds. They are also great scavengers and will find a road killed rabbit in no time. When I saw these two feeding on a carcass during heavy rain, I thought it would be interesting to photograph them looking so damp and dishevelled.

Like oranges packed tightly in a box, and glistening from a recent shower, the bright berries of the Cuckoo-pint stand out wonderfully at the edge of a woodland.

WHAT'S A BLACKBERRY *by Gordon D'Arcy*

"Don't touch that! A dog might have peed on it," came the exhortation from the little girl with the big glasses. "Look, he's eating it," she continued, disgust written all over her face.

The field trip leader raised his hand, calling for attention.

"Would you please put that gameboy back into your backpack…and you, yes you," he insisted, pointing to a neatly dressed eight year old with a bewildered facial expression, "Put that mobile away. How many times do you have to be told?"

Realizing he was coming across too strongly, too teacherly, he added lightly, "I can't tell the difference between your ring tone and a kingfisher."

The subsequent sniggering caught the leader by surprise but seeing it as an opportunity to garner support, he smiled broadly. The twenty young heads turned towards the man with the binoculars wondering what he might tell them next.

"This, boys and girls, is a blackberry bush…"

Over the top? Everybody knows a briar. Don't they? This would never happen on a field outing in Ireland, green Ireland. Would it? I'm afraid it would, has and does regularly. This kind of unawareness, is all too common nowadays in rural Ireland. Nor is this entirely my own experience: I have discussed this issue with many colleagues, working like me, in the field of environmental education. Indeed some have placed the phenomenon in the context of a general and increasing breakdown in connectedness with the countryside - a relationship that the same children's parents (grandparents, more likely), and countless generations before them, took for granted.

If this phenomenon is true, what is causing it; what are the factors giving rise to it, given that most pre-teenage children (from my experience) are self confident, naturally curious, and refreshingly keen to get involved in all sorts of pursuits?

One could ask the children, and I often do, especially when I see them ostensibly engaged in some nature project. I look for their reaction to handling natural items - leaves, birds' nests, mini-beasts etc. Engagement ranges from utterly 'hands-on' (rare enough) to being satisfied with an arms-length look and a bit of info. Disappointing, yes, and not what someone of my generation would expect of the present one. In a way, however, such voyeurism is unfair, since the causes are clearly extraneous and not the result of some intrinsic change in the nature of childhood. If anything children are more willing to experiment, more avant-garde than formerly.

Diminished exposure to the outdoors must be a primary factor. Children, in the main, no longer walk to school. Is this because they don't want to? In some instances, perhaps. But having frequently walked and talked with children along some quiet bohereen or other, on a school outing, and seen them joyfully engaged, I do not think so. I often ask for a show of hands on the question of walking to school and even in the most rural areas, only a small percentage actually commute in this manner. A few (very few) cycle, but as a means of becoming environmentally aware, this is not the same as walking. Nor is playing in the garden a substitute. Yes, there is exposure here to nature but it is 'tame' nature - manicured lawn, meticulously attended flower borders, tarmac driveway and, as often as not, sterile Leyland Cypress hedge.

A primary reason for the ferry-to-school syndrome is obviously and understandably the avoidance of danger. Parental anxiety in the normal stress-filled day simply won't allow for the risks associated with walking along our increasingly busy roads. The danger of accident, from speeding cars, motorcycles, farm transport, even from animals, is real. Annual accident statistics include one or two particularly tragic reports of a child killed - running out from behind a school bus, chasing a football into the road from the playground, or some other such highly avoidable incident.

Another concern is the threat from paedophilia. Abominable as this social scourge is, its prevalence, in terms of head of population is low. In certain circumstances, unaccompanied children, even in groups, may be vulnerable but the incidence is rare, and, if comparisons are appropriate, it is certainly less a threat than that of speeding vehicles. The potential for this kind of harm, in transit to or from school, nevertheless looms large in the anxiety list of many parents. Despite the additional strain attendant on being constantly 'there' for their children, parents gain significant peace of mind in personally transporting their offspring to and from their places of work and play. The fact that they themselves, in so doing, might become part of the perennial accident problem, is a tragic irony, often overlooked in the analysis. This expediency is a product of our modern way of work: up early, dash to school, crèche, or other 'holding facility', en route to work: home at all hours to accommodate the expensive, usually complex guardianship arrangement worked out at the beginning of term. The children may be missing out, their exposure to the wider world sacrificed, independence and initiative stultified, sense of place unrealised, etc. etc. - but aren't they safe?

The demand for physical well-being is incontestable, but what is being sacrificed, even denied in the process? Without really monitoring such change or debating its ramifications the present adult generation is inadvertently presiding over the profound environmental disengagement of our school-going youth. Children are being brought from one hermetically sealed situation (the house), to another (the school), by way of a third (the car). They are thus denied exposure to the otherness, the richness, and the adventure potential of their parish. They are growing through their most formative pre-teenage years without really engaging with nature; seeing it often as a mere backdrop or an inconsequential aside. Nature for many, in fact, is a DVD of the Serengeti, or a Discovery Channel documentary.

Not that this should be condemned. In the absence of an adequate supply of home-grown nature programmes on RTE and other popular media channels, here is at least a global perspective on the wonderful world of nature. Ironically this can be counterproductive, resulting in local nature being seen as ordinary, in comparison. Nature is not on your doorstep: it is something you travel abroad to see.

RTE radio's 'Mooney Goes Wild' is a striking exception. Here the emphasis is both national and local. The quarter of a million listeners who tune in every Saturday morning are testimony to the public hunger for such a cleverly produced nature forum. The annual, nation-wide dawn chorus event, inviting the participation of thousands of enthusiasts of all ages, is both a celebration of the wonderful natural phenomenon of birdsong and of modern radio broadcasting.

As an example of our growing disconnectedness with nature we need look no further than trees. Most children cannot identify even our most common species. They are simply not taught about trees, other than in the context of their importance for timber, or the gaseous exchange process - in geography and science. Trees are represented mainly as the source of raw material, important to the economy or to human health. Not holistically.

It was not always so, however. Experts disagree nowadays on the degree to which trees featured in Gaelic education but it is common knowledge that, children learned the Irish alphabet through their names. This may have been a hangover from prehistory when individual trees, groves and forests were afforded sacred status. We learn also that the 'caste' Gaelic society was ranked - from nobles (Airig fedo) to slaves (Losa- fedo) - in accordance with categories of native trees: high value trees, the oak - to shrubs, the bramble.

Inauguration sites were located beside prominent, venerable trees used in the ritual. Indeed, in inter-clan rivalry, maximum insult was gained by cutting down the bile tree of an enemy. The law tracts, poems, triads and other contemporary references point to the various uses to which trees could be put, and fines were imposed for cutting them down without permission.

Though the Gaelic Irish were far from being a nation of 'tree-huggers', the abundance of arboreal placenames surviving to the present points clearly to a one-time profound connectedness with trees. Places were named by the 'look' various trees gave to the landscape. A large number of the tree placenames survive, many in situations that are no longer wooded. Agricultural expansionism during the ring-fort phase of the early medieval period saw widespread tree clearance, indicating ultimate victory of the practical over the aesthetic. There is a sense, nonetheless, that Gaelic Ireland did not regard the forest as hostile, a place to avoid, to be wary of, as was the case in many other parts of northern Europe during the medieval period. Indeed, during the wars that saw the final collapse of the Gaelic regime, the woods became the retreat and sanctuary to Irish kerne, much to the chagrin of the forces of the new order. A major colonial priority was to clear remaining woods, not simply for use in the burgeoning new industries of the time, but also to remove the practical and spiritual sanctuary that they represented. That was then: this is now. What relevance today?

One of history's irreplaceable functions is to give a nation a sense of itself; of how it came to be, of the values that make it what it is. For the present to point us confidently toward the future it must awaken in us aspects of the past that are essentially of us. Given that the past decade has seen more change in Ireland than the past century; in economic growth, in evolving multiculturalism, the Irish language remains intrinsic. Essentially a rural language, it is struggling to survive in our increasingly urbanized society where commerce favours the versatility of English. The constant updating of what is essentially an ancient tongue with incongruous, 'filler-words' (analogous perhaps to the replacement of many former oakwoods with alien but commercially important spruce plantations) frustrates

those seeking authenticity from our heritage.

Nature and language can be combined, however, in a positive, optimistic sense, in the naming of our animals and plants, infusing both with new life. Indeed, a meaningful heritage connection can be forged, helping to promote both the language and our former close connection with nature. With trees this is straightforward since we have barely two-dozen native species, located often in our hedgerows and copses. These can readily be pointed out in the course of a field trip. A follow-up lesson in the class combining the various strands of natural history and language can be used to develop the subject.

Modern Ireland seems impatient with old values. Heritage appreciation, requiring quietude and reflection, is unfashionable in our world of novelty and distraction. The catchphrase 'going forward' has been adopted, it seems, by any and all wishing to promote a dynamic agenda. Few, if any of us, would want to return to Gaelic times, marked as they were by internecine feuding, cattle rustling and a far from fair, conservative social regime. One characteristic of the times, however, that comes down to us through the literature, which we undoubtedly have lost, is affection for nature. This was unselfconsciously expressed in the rich corpus of lore about flora and fauna. Trees were especially celebrated. In Sweeney's Lay (Laoi Shuibhne), for instance, the language reflects this intimacy with trees. A dozen trees and shrubs are exuberantly praised for their being and their beauty. This is how he describes the lowly blackberry, "O briar, little arched one, Thou grantest no fair terms, Thou ceasest not to tear me, Till thou hast thy fill of blood." Here affection has become enchantment. Through the vehicle of the nature verse we encounter a pantheistic spiritualism, a spiritualism initially embraced, later rejected by Christianity. Sweeney finishes defiantly, "My aversion in woods - I conceal it not from anyone - is the leafy stirk of an oak swaying evermore."

P.W.Joyce (Irish Names of Places, 1902) cites Drish, Drishane, Drisheen, Drishoge, Drishaghaun and a host of compounds and suffixes, all derived from the Irish word Dris, for blackberry or briar. A high proportion emanate from topographical or natural features or from the names of birds and animals. The names resonate not only with familiarity but also with the affection expressed in Sweeney's Lay. Mac tire (son of the land) an alternative name for the wolf (mentioned in a poem in the Book of Leinster), and found occasionally in place names, is a case in point. Compare this with the wolf's status as symbol of odium to the colonists in the early modern period: principal public enemies - 'wolfe and woodkerne.'

Nowadays that sense of affection, with the whole of the natural world, is teetering. It has been replaced mainly by indifference, but also by a kind of 'selective' sentimentality - "We all love the robin; he'd nearly take the food out of your hand"... A lack of understanding of basic ecological principals can further complicate the issue - "If I had my way I'd kill every magpie; there's not a songbird in the garden while they are about."

One of the reasons for the abundance of magpies, of course, is that we no longer have many big birds of prey that would hunt them. Historically, the disappearance of raptors has been linked to estate management and the predator control exercised by gamekeepers. Indeed, our new-found passion for gardening (witness the growth of gardening centres throughout the country), ostensibly a green, hands-on engagement with nature, is also about order and control. We seem to be uncomfortable with natural 'untidiness' - the rotting log, dandelions growing in with the flowers, leaves on the path. In general most of us approve of nature - but on our terms.

Field outings are revealing in another, rather disturbing, way. Aside from the occasional child with a disability (usually assisted by a special-needs teacher or a relative), who in fact often demonstrates an heroic 'gung-ho' attitude in keeping up, increasingly a clique of laggards is to be found at the tail of the group. These usually overweight and unfit children - of both sexes - distinguish themselves further in their capacity to draw attention to themselves. "I've left my lunch in

the classroom." (Yes, that was the idea). "There are no shops out here." (Yes, I knew that also). "Are we there yet?"(!). Teachers confide that such children live sedentary life-styles, don't participate enthusiastically in any sport, are often addicted to computers, and usually come from domestic circumstances where they are cosseted and where inactivity is the norm. Many national schools have introduced a healthy-eating regime and on one day per week children are asked not to bring such unhealthy fare as crisps, chocolate bars, and fizzy drinks for their school lunch. Such schools are to be commended for this enlightened approach. It will undoubtedly make a difference, especially when it is combined with an awareness programme. The Green Flag initiative, designed to encourage national schools in promoting environmental awareness has begun to make a real impact. About 55 per cent, more than 2,000, of the Republic's national schools are involved and the number grows annually. Besides supporting improved eating habits in our pre-teenage population, the programme focuses on litter control in the playground, recycling, caring for nature, and working to increase environmental awareness in and around the school. It is not easy to gain the prestigious flag. Evidence of real commitment is required, from teachers and pupils, and once obtained the flag may be retained only under similar stipulations. The initiative's great strength is its emphasis on respect - personal respect in the context of one's place of work and perhaps more importantly, abstract respect for the environment and, by extension, society at large.

There are other environmental initiatives helping to raise awareness in schools, many of which are championed by the Environmental Information Centre, ENFO. This organization acts as a distribution centre for an impressive range of environmental material including work packs, posters, books, pamphlets, videos, DVDs, and much more. National schools throughout the country are constantly circulated with material from ENFO. However, due to the enormous predominance of daily 'junk-mail' received by each school through the post, necessitating rapid sorting, it does not always receive the attention it should.

A scheme that has impacted enormously since it was introduced as a pilot in 1997 is the Heritage in Schools Scheme. The brainchild of retired principal Leo Hallissey, a cooperative venture between the Heritage Council and the INTO, the scheme has revolutionised environmental education throughout the Republic. Where formerly children relied on the vision and enthusiasm of individual teachers for such learning, this new scheme is structured so that a specialist from a panel of about 130 visits the school bringing some particular heritage skill to the pupils. Heritage is a broad church and the contributions range from folklore to basket making, from archaeology to ancient musical instruments. The majority of specialists and visits, however, relate to some aspect or other of the natural world. The specialist may spend the day in the classroom or on a field trip. The focus is usually on a particular topic or treatment. In all circumstances the teacher is in attendance. The scheme succeeds because it answers a need, occasionally but not usually satisfied by the teacher, who is invariably overstretched anyway. Everybody gains from the experience, the chief beneficiaries, of course, being the pupils. In its first year there were a mere 15 visits but this has now been increased to about 1500 visits per annum and more than 60,000 children have been reached.

Teachers, gracious enough to allow know-it-all specialists into their classrooms, are enthusiastically supporting the scheme for the sake of the broader education of their charges. They, more than anyone, have noted the change in how children come to and go home from school and their diminishing exposure to heritage. They recognize also that there are gains for society at large in facilitating the stimulation of young minds in directions other than that of competitive achievement and in values other than those of crude economic gain.

Humphrey O'Sullivan, whose diaries (1827-1835) provide us with extraordinary insights into Irish country life in the years preceding the famine, exemplifies the dedicated master working stoically under what would nowadays be described as impossible circumstances.

Originally a hedge-schoolteacher (redolent of the erudite, rag-taggle character in Brian Friel's 'Translations'), O'Sullivan set up school in a turf cabin in Callan, in 1808 (having taken over from his father), though through dogged fundraising and influence managed eventually to acquire a permanent building. He taught in Callan until 1824.

He must have been a wonderful teacher for his diaries, written entirely in Irish, reveal both a scholarly curiosity and a wide interest in contemporary events, which he undoubtedly passed on to his pupils. He recorded major disasters, political rallies, faction fights, etc. His deep compassion for the terrible plight of starving parishioners is evident and he was acutely aware of impending famine. At heart, however, O'Sullivan was a naturalist. He noticed and noted countryside plants, animals and birds (several of which are now either rare or completely gone, not only from Kilkenny but from Ireland). A lover of the Irish language, he took pains to record the various Irish names of particular species, distinguishing, for instance, between the Heron, the Crane and the Bittern with a total of seven names. He was fascinated by the sounds that birds made, noting phonetically the monotonous calls of quails (fuid fuide) and corncrakes, (aic aic), then common inhabitants of the fields around Callan. "There are many words [in Irish] for the whistling of the birds, the fluting (scolgaire) of the blackbird, the crowing (glaodhach), of the cock, the cackling, (gragadghail) of the hen, the cawing (grag) of the rook, the cuckooing (cuach aireacht) of the cuckoo." Undoubtedly he spent days with his pupils in the field - when the weather was good. Nowadays, even where the teacher is predisposed to the 'outdoor classroom', there seem to be innumerable obstacles discouraging the practice.

O'Sullivan has been seen as an Irish counterpart to Gilbert White, whose famous *Natural History of Selborne* (1789) provides us with a vivid nature diary from rural England's Romantic period. Indeed, he may well have been influenced by White's work. However, the diary form, of which there is apparently no Irish tradition, is incidental: O'Sullivan's legacy is the linking of nature and language in the Gaelic tradition, providing contemporary Ireland with a unique literary stepping stone to more connected times.

Not long ago, I was accompanied by a local national schoolteacher (and pupils), to the site of a 19th century hedge-school near Lough Conn in County Mayo. The site, alongside a country bohereen was simply a wide hollow behind the ditch. Though dry and cosy (for cattle), it was inconceivable that this was once a classroom. The place was highly evocative: you could almost hear the rote chant of the children and the intermittent instruction of the master, huddled in the shelter of their whitethorn bower - a far cry from the comfortable, IT rigged classrooms of the present day.

I am of the generation that thought nothing of walking to and from school. It was something that everybody did. It was safe. I left home, often early, usually alone and approached, with reluctance, the confines of the school. The walk was the highlight of my day. I suppose it was my daydreaming temperament that, once exposed, allowed me to indulge my passion for nature, a passion it must be said not shared by all my schoolmates. I was not a recluse, however. I also enjoyed the horseplay, the 'war'-games, the building of ditch forts and tree lookouts.

As time passed I became aware of the change in the weather and the seasons by the look of the sky through the hedges. I learned where reliable shelter from showers could be found. I knew when and where to look for birds' nests. I learned their calls and songs by catching glimpses of the birds as they sang. I could distinguish between various animal footprints in a muddy puddle and recognized the distinctive scent left by a fox on a gatepost the night before. I overcame fears triggered by the bizarre close-up world of the roadside - watching a spider wrap up a hapless insect for later consumption, examining a squashed frog, its entrails glistening in the dewy morning, treating nettle stings with dock-leaves.

I ate blackberries.

Gordon D'Arcy is a naturalist, author and artist. He is involved in environmental education, particularly at primary level, visiting some 80 schools per annum, many under the Heritage in Schools Scheme. He also teaches at third level in NUIG and the Burren College of Art.
He has written seven books on various aspects of the natural world including, 'The Guide to the Birds of Ireland', (Irish Wildlife Publications, 1981), 'The Natural History of the Burren' (Immel, 1992) and most recently, 'The Burren Wall', (Tir Eolas, 2006), and contributed chapters to a number of others.
He has had about ten solo exhibitions, mainly on wildlife themes, most recently in Kenny's Gallery, Galway.

Vivid colours stretch across
the sky and a soft mist forms
on the ground as a bright
day comes to an end during
the winter months.

Two different views of the same thing. Above, Common Reeds at the edge of a lagoon catch the light of the evening sun in autumn. In the bottom image, I recorded the movement of the reeds in summer, during an unseasonable gale, to create a completely abstract image

Redpolls are regular visitors to feeders in a friend's garden during the wintertime. I captured this portrait as one paused briefly on a branch in the strong light of a clear, sunny afternoon.

When I saw a small flock of Twite landing on some barbed wire I felt
that it made a lovely contrast. This rare and delicate bird sitting on the
harsh and jagged wire that is all too common in our countryside.

I came across this Irish Hare on a piece of scrubland. Slightly backlit with late winter sunshine, it paused briefly to allow me to make this portrait before running off to find cover.

Yellow Loosestrife brightens up the flat grasslands of the Shannon Callows on a bright summer morning. This peaceful landscape is a hive of activity during the spring and summer with many birds choosing to rear their young in the deep vegetation.

A Sedge Warbler brings a juicy red caterpillar to its waiting chicks.

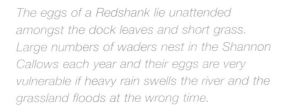

The Linnet with its brightly coloured breast is one of the many birds that thrive in the callows.

The eggs of a Redshank lie unattended amongst the dock leaves and short grass. Large numbers of waders nest in the Shannon Callows each year and their eggs are very vulnerable if heavy rain swells the river and the grassland floods at the wrong time.

A Curlew lifts her head to check for danger as she incubates her eggs.

The striking Garden Tiger is a large and common moth found all over Ireland. The spots and blotches on the wings vary and no two moths are exactly the same.

This Small Copper butterfly was resting on the ground during a dull spell one morning. Although it remained stationary while I photographed it, as soon as the sun reappeared it flew off to feed.

A Zebra Spider devours its prey. These spiders do not build a web but instead lurk in the undergrowth and leap on prey items that land nearby.

A pair of Common Blue damselflies couple at the edge of a small freshwater pool.

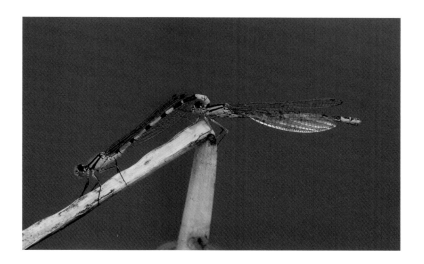

The strangely named Pebble Prominent moth is common and I found this one resting on the underside of some discarded pallets in my garden. I didn't notice it at first as it blended so well with the old worn wood.

On a beautiful summer day in the Burren, I came across this Whitethroat bringing food to its hungry chicks. It was an expert collector as this image shows, getting caterpillars, spiders and flies all in one mouthful.

In the last light of a June evening I witnessed three Pine Marten kittens playing on the roof of a derelict cottage in County Galway. The next day I spent long hours sitting hidden nearby and although I got some lovely portraits of the kittens individually, they did not appear together for me.

NATURE'S BEST *by Richard Collins*

Seven wonders of the Irish animal world
An encounter with an iconic creature in the wild is an unforgettable experience; one has the feeling of being blessed by the gods. Nowadays, our affluent nature lovers want to see Great White Sharks in the Southern oceans or Birds of Paradise in the jungles of New Guinea. When I was young, however, our yearnings were more modest. The creatures we longed to glimpse were closer to hand but they were no less exotic for all that.

The Tree Cat

In the Limerick of the 1950's, the local celebrity animal was the Pine Marten. I had little idea what this mysterious beast looked like, or even how big it was, but the name had an exotic ring to it and so this creature had to be something special. A teacher spoke of Martens in hushed tones. Being so rare, they had something of the mystique of the Abominable Snowman, the mysterious beast which featured prominently in news reports before Everest was conquered.

The last few Irish Pine Martens lived on the fringes of the Burren in County Clare about 25 miles from where I grew up but a sighting of this secretive nocturnal beast was considered as likely as meeting a ghost. Indeed Martens were credited with quasi-supernatural powers; they would have you sussed long before you could lay eyes on them. It would be another 30 years before I had the privilege of seeing the 'cat crainn' in the wild; at Mota Quay, on the banks of the Shannon in county Tipperary, as I slipped a ring onto a Willow Warbler's leg in the early morning, the elusive beast emerged from the forest and ran past me. With its longish legs, it did look a bit like a cat.

Salt on the tail

If the Pine Marten was the rarest wild animal around, the commonest, when I was a child, was the Rabbit.

Mysterious creatures are not necessarily rare and, at that time, Rabbits overran the country. My grandparents' farms in Limerick and Clare teemed with bunnies and, to a child from the city, they were loveable little beasts. How I longed to stroke and cuddle one of those endearing balls of fur. If you shook salt on a Rabbit's tail, I was told, it would surrender. So I carried salt in a matchbox when visiting the warrens and waited patiently at the mouths of burrows, to no avail.

The story of the Rabbit in Ireland is a curious one. Natives of Spain, they attracted the attention of the invading Romans. Soon they were being cosseted in artificial warrens surrounded by moats; bunnies can swim but, like pussy cats, they hate getting wet. Roman farmers bred strains which produced large, and frequent, litters. Bunnies have been 'breeding like rabbits' ever since.

Rabbits did not reach Ireland until after the Norman invasion. The new conquerors established the first warrens here. Then some bunnies escaped, setting up colonies in the wild and attacking the farmer's crops. They ate more grass than his livestock.

Rabbits, not being great runners, hide when danger threatens. Their safe havens are underground. It's this secret underground society aspect of his life which gives the bunny his mystique. Although we know a bit more nowadays about the morals and mores of Rabbits, there is still much to be learned about life in the warren.

Rabbits sometimes live as monogamous pairs, each with its own burrow. In large colonies, however, groups of bucks make loose wife-swapping arrangements with the local does. There may be up to 20 animals in a coalition and several coalitions in a colony. The dominant does breed at the centre of the warren, with the less privileged ones relegated to the edge. Kittens born to high status does tend to do better in life than those of lower rank. Whether in a colony or not, each doe will have her own nest chamber, the entrance to which she blocks with soil whenever she leaves. The kittens are fed, for about five minutes, once a day, but Rabbit milk is extraordinarily nourishing.

Bunnies may be cute and cuddly but they are not without their dark side. A doe will attack, and even kill, any kitten she encounters which is not her own. Such a baby may compete with hers for scarce resources, so it benefits her family to kill it. A buck never attacks babies. It would be against his genetic interests to do so; males are promiscuous, so any kitten could be a buck's own offspring or closely related to him.

The Porpoise

On childhood visits to the seaside, I would hear accounts of mysterious black and white creatures, called 'sea-pigs'. I had never seen one of these exotic animals and they took on all the mystique of mermaids. One morning, as I swam off the beach at Ballybunion in a calm sea with a large swell, there they were, just a few metres away between the rollers, three black forms with crescent-shaped fins. I was thrilled and terrified. I've been fascinated by porpoises and dolphins ever since.

'Sea-pig' is a translation of the Irish 'muc mhara'. 'Porpoise' comes from the Latin 'porcus', a pig, and 'piscis', a fish, an apt name for this fat little character. Porpoises never jump clear of the water the way dolphins do and they don't race the bow-waves of ships. They rest by floating on the surface and, apparently, never sleep.

The Goldcrest of the whales, the Porpoise is the smallest Irish cetacean. A female might be 1.9 metres long, males being smaller. Size matters when it comes to survival in cold environments. A small cetacean can live on prey which would not sustain a larger one, but small creatures need more food, proportionately, than big ones; small bodies lose heat more quickly in the cold sea. Baby whales are much more vulnerable than

their parents and they lack the thick layers of blubber which protects adults from the cold. The bigger a baby is, the better it can cope with cold, so Porpoises have large babies, between a quarter and one third as heavy as their mothers.

But producing a large baby is a drain on a mother's resources and she can't afford to do so very often. Porpoises start breeding when they are three or four years old and they breed every two to four years or so thereafter. A female will produce only three or four young during her life.

The low birth rate leaves Porpoises with a very small margin of births over deaths. This was not a problem in the past, because the life expectancy of sea mammals was high. The threats posed by Killer Whales, and possibly Bottle-nosed Dolphins, were manageable. Now, however, Man has introduced new dangers.

Porpoises are attracted to fish struggling in nets. Modern monofilament nets are almost invisible to them, nor can they be detected by a Porpoise's echolocation system. The hapless sea-pigs become entangled in the invisible webs and drown. Like many whale species, Porpoises can become disoriented and end up stranded on beaches. It is odd that such intelligent creatures come to grief in this way and nobody can explain why they do. Perhaps pollutants have sickened such animals.

Monster of the deep

Among the many places I have visited, none has the appeal of those two jagged Alpine peaks projecting from the sea west of Valentia; the Skellig rocks. There at the foot of the dark rock, I once encountered, just a few metres away, the Atlantic's biggest fish, the Basking Shark.

Specimens can be up to 10 metres long. Only the whale shark is bigger. The two giants have similar lifestyles but the Whale Shark likes warm tropical waters whereas the Basking prefers cooler temperate seas.

The Basking Shark has an enormous gape. With mouth wide open, it moves through the water, like a giant vacuum cleaner, its gills trapping plankton. Thus, the Atlantic's largest creature feeds exclusively on some of the smallest, the main items in the diet being copepods, little crustaceans. The shark still has teeth, inherited from its voracious ancestors, but these are tiny, rendered redundant through natural selection. This great beast is docile, totally harmless and not too fearful of humans. Divers occasionally approach and swim with Basking Sharks.

The life-cycle of the giant fish is still a bit of a mystery. Until comparatively recently, it was not even known if the shark laid eggs or produced live young. Then, in 1936, one caught off Norway gave birth to five babies while being towed into port. Male sharks have a pair of copulatory organs, called claspers, and fertilisation is internal. The eggs hatch within the body of the female but the young are not born for about three and a half years. Sharks have no equivalent of a mammal's placenta, however; the eggs, and the young which hatch from them, are retained only as a protection against predators.

At the beginning of the 19th Century, the basking shark was one of the mainstays of the Irish sea-fishing industry. Only the herring was more important as a prey species. The huge dorsal fin of the shark protrudes from the water and, in calm weather, a fish is easy to spot. Fishermen would approach the shark quietly, in a small boat, and plunge a harpoon with a rope attached to it, into the fish. It could take several hours for an exhausted shark to be captured. The enormous liver would be removed and boiled in cauldrons to extract oil. This would be sold as fuel to power lamps, streetlights in cities and the lanterns of lighthouses.

Shark fishing was revived off Achill at the end of the Second World War, when industrial oils became scarce. Up to a thousand sharks were killed annually, 1,800 being caught during 1952 alone. The Achill fishery closed in the mid 1970s.

The 'Jay-thrush'

Ireland has Song Thrushes, Mistle Thrushes, Redwings and Fieldfares but, in Limerick, we also had the Jay-thrush. The dark brown Jays, with their beautiful blue design on the wing and gleaming white rumps, were not thrushes, however. They were crows.

Jays are the London cabbies of the bird world. The cabby must master what's known as 'the knowledge'; he has to become completely au fait with the geography of his enormous city. The Jay likewise performs the most astonishing feats of memory.

These avian Alfred Beits and Chester Beattys don't collect paintings and manuscripts but they do gather nuts and seeds. Their speciality is acorns. Collecting begins in September and Jays spend up to ten hours per day collecting and storing. A single bird will gather 4,500 to 5,000 acorns each autumn and travel up to 6km with them to storage sites. The nuts are held in the crop, a sort of handbag in the bird's neck. They carry about three per journey, but as many as nine have been recorded. Each acorn is buried at a separate location in the ground. The nut is pushed into the soil, hammered a few times and covered with leaf litter or moss.

Collecting acorns is hard work but not that demanding mentally. But laying you hands, or beak, on acorns stored in 5,000 different locations, when times are tough in the middle of winter, five months after you buried them, is another matter. Our Jay does exactly that. The London cab-driver's exam would be chicken-feed, or Jay feed, to him. Not only does he memorise all that geographical information, he can find his caches unerringly in winter when the leaves are gone from the trees and the landscape is radically changed. Jays retrieve their acorns even when they are covered by 40cms of snow!

But what do the oaks think of all this thieving? As it happens, they rather welcome it. Taking acorns is not really theft, it is more like a business arrangement or a DIRT tax. The jay is a sort of sub-contractor to the oak.

Oaks need to have their seeds planted well away in suitable soil, a service which the Jay provides. A Jay won't recover all of his stored nuts and some will die without retrieving theirs. You could say that the Jay leaves the seeds to the oak in its will! The oak sacrifices some seeds to the Jay, but gets a distribution service in return; 'if you scratch my back, I'll scratch yours'.

Bohemians

The winter of 1962/3 was particularly severe. The cotoneasters in our front garden had a rich crop of berries and, one morning, a flock of birds arrived and started to feed on them. But these were no ordinary visitors. Larger than Chaffinches but much smaller than Starlings, the little acrobats had chestnut-coloured crests, black bibs and face-masks. Their tails had bright yellow tips. They produced a chorus of soft high-pitched tinkling calls, like water in a fountain.

It was a while before we discovered that they were called 'Waxwings'. Had they come all the way from Sweden or Finland? Were they refugees from Siberia, that remote and forbidding place? The prospect gave the Waxwings an added mystique; Limerick had the largest religious confraternity in the world and we knew that Siberia was full of concentration camps operated by evil atheistic communists!

Waxwings only visit us occasionally, at least in any numbers. They prefer to spend the winter nearer home but, every now and then, they 'erupt'; flocks burst forth from their Nordic forests and head south. Once in a decade or so, there is what are called a 'Waxwing year' and they arrive in force.

In Europe, the Waxwing was known as the 'bohemian jay'. Its erratic arrivals and departures resembled the wanderings of the gypsies, who were thought to hail from Bohemia. Gypsies have, in fact, no special connection with Bohemia. They left India for the Middle East around the 3rd Century AD. Their arrival in Europe during the 15th Century, was a kind of eruption, so perhaps referring to Waxwings as 'bohemians' is

appropriate. The bird is still called the 'Bohemian Waxwing' in America. The English name refers to the red markings on the bird's wings, which resemble sealing wax.

But why do Waxwings have such an erratic lifestyle? The answer has to do with food shortages. In winter, they rely on berries. During mild sunny summers, the trees have a bumper crop. There are plenty of berries during the following winter and the Waxwings thrive. But if the weather is poor throughout a summer, the trees produce few berries. The Waxwings face a sudden famine, so they head south.

This is not migration in the ordinary sense. Waxwings seem to move randomly in their search for fruit and berries. A bird ringed in Poland, for instance, turned up in Eastern Siberia, 5,500 kilometres away, the following winter. When they find food, they gorge themselves; a Waxwing, observed in Norfolk in 1957, ate 390 berries in two and a half hours. This was about its own weight in food!

Lampers

As a child, I had an inordinate fear of a strange creature lurking in the depths of the Shannon. It was known as the 'lamper eel' and it lived, we thought, by drinking blood. Swimming in the river, your leg might brush against water weed or a floating piece of debris. Horror of horrors! Could it be the dreaded lamper? The mysterious beast would seek out the soft flesh of a thigh. Its huge circular mouth would lock onto the leg, its ring of sharp teeth opening a deep wound. Then it would start to suck. Nothing could dislodge the horrible vampire, except fire. You would have to leave the water, with the wriggling snake-like creature dangling from you. Only a lighted match applied to its belly would persuade the lamper to let go.

There was, in fact, no risk whatsoever of falling victim to such a beast while swimming in the Shannon, or anywhere else. Lampreys exploit fish, not mammals, although Sea Lampreys will occasionally lock onto a Porpoise.

Lampreys are not related to eels although they look superficially like them. In evolutionary terms, the two are poles apart. The name 'lamprey' comes from the Latin 'lamper', to lick and 'petra', a rock, as in Simon Peter. Licking rocks is, presumably, what the old naturalists thought lampreys did for a crust. The description is not far wide of the mark; the female Sea Lamprey lifts stones from river bottoms with her huge sucker mouth. She is not searching for food, however, but preparing a bed in which to lay her eggs. Her babies have no teeth and their eyes are covered with skin. They burrow in the mud at the bottoms of rivers and live by filtering debris from the water. When four or five years old, their eyes and teeth develop and they become adults.

Most adults head downstream to the sea, but a few stay on in the lakes and rivers. Adult lampreys live off fish, sucking their fluids and soft tissues and leaving characteristic circular wounds on their victims. An anti-coagulant prevents the victim's blood from clotting. Sea Lampreys return to the rivers to spawn. They stop feeding during the journey upstream and their digestive systems degenerate. They die soon after spawning.

Our smallest Irish species, the Brook Lamprey, lives its entire life in rivers and lakes. It may have been introduced here. There is a theory, however, that it's not a distinct species but only a non-migratory form of the River Lamprey. Brook Lampreys are filter feeders. They don't suck the blood of fish.

Lampreys need clean waters in which to spawn. Pollution and the drainage of rivers now threaten Limerick's equivalent of the Lough Ness Monster.

Richard Collins is a zoologist known for his work on Mute Swans. An experienced broadcaster, he is part of RTE Radio 1's Mooney Goes Wild on One team. A former Honorary Secretary of BirdWatch Ireland, he writes a weekly column for the Irish Examiner, reviews books for the Sunday Business Post and lectures in the Adult Education Department UCD.

Coots are very territorial and regularly get into skirmishes. These two were photographed having a minor spat on Lough Corrib.

The sun sets over the Terraun wetlands in County Offaly. Wetlands are vital resources for a large number of our birds and also for many insects and plants.

A Little Grebe settles down to incubate her eggs on a nest made up of loose reeds and grasses. If an intruder upsets the adult bird it will quickly cover the eggs with this vegetation before leaving the nest until the danger has passed.

The bright blue flowers of the Water Forget-me-not catch the light of the summer sunshine.

To freeze the motion of the wings of this Common Hawker dragonfly would require a complicated high speed flash set up, probably in captive situation. However, sometimes they hover almost motionless, except for their swiftly beating wings, and I decided to try make an image of this.

A perfect Spiders web covered in dew catches the light of the rising sun.

During the winter months this small waterfall is a raging torrent but in the dry months of summer it is reduced to a few tiny bands of water.

(left) I was concealed in a hide on the shore of Lough Derg when this Cormorant came close and started exhibiting some interesting behaviour. It would dip its head into the water and pick up clumps of lily pads and weeds and start shaking them. Whether this had a purpose or the bird was simply having fun I still don't know.

Taking an extremely close-up view of a Common Spotted Orchid reveals the intricate patterns and shapes in the petals.

This Common Sandpiper was incubating eggs on its nest tucked under a bush at the side of a small river in County Kerry.

The Wood White is a delicate butterfly with gossamer thin wings and a long narrow body unlike the more sturdy white butterflies which frequent our gardens. It lives and breeds in quiet sheltered places and flutters along in an almost feeble manner, frequently stopping on plants to rest and feed.

Cuckoos are famous for their parasitic behaviour of laying their eggs in other birds nests and leaving the host bird to rear their young. I have seen them many times on trees, rocks and walls singing their familiar song. However, I had never seen one eat. After a tip-off from a friend I was able to get this image of one feeding on grubs. It would work its way down a line of fence posts occasionally dropping down onto the field and returning to the post with its catch.

(Overleaf) *A vivid sunset over the limestone pavements of the Burren, one of Ireland's most spectacular landscapes.*

SEASONS *by Damien Enright*

SPRING

Wild May weather and, in the garden, the rotary clothes dryer and its cargo spins like a hurdy-gurdy full of children at a fairground; one can almost hear their shrieks of delight. High overhead, two swallows swing about the sky. Their wings are half closed, like ice skaters with their hands behind their backs to lessen drag.

Outside my work-room window, sunlight sweeps across the lawn and everything shines. "Rough winds do strip the darling leaves of May..." to paraphrase the bard. New-born and pastel green, they fly horizontally from the high beeches but, happily, fresh buds will open to replace them. In October, we will have to sweep them all up - where then for the rough winds of May?!

Now, the floor of the local woods is acre-to-acre blue and white, with not a square yard of green showing. For bluebell watchers, water-colourists or suckers for sylvan scenes, this is the time to go wood-walking. Bluebells are at their densest; the very light beneath the trees is blue. White mats of ramsons compete, wild garlic so-called. The woods smell like pungent Italian kitchens.

By evening, the wind has dropped and there is a universal stillness. The bay is like glass. The inshore waters, reflecting the colours of the village houses, are splashed with shades of red, orange, blue and green. A single dwelling has made a fire; the smoke is a grey, upright column against the woods behind it. Nothing stirs; one might be looking at a photograph. Painted boats float on a painted sea.

Then, the ripple of a shoal of mullet suddenly breaks the surface. The world comes alive. A cow moos mournfully across the bay. A dog barks. My spaniel plunges into the water with a loud splash. I hear children whooping in some distant garden. I move on.

It has been a weekend of 'pet' days and, next morning, sitting above a cove where there is no sign of Man or trace of human time, I while away an hour, drinking in the spring sunlight and watching a dozen gannets quartering the air. Huge and white, back and forth they fly, fifty feet over the sea, in pairs or squadrons. Spotting the sand eel shoals, they rise like parabolas against the blue, pause for a second at the apex, then rocket down into their midst.

From the cliff above, their trajectories underwater are like white torpedoes; they travel three metres or more by the force of the dive. Seconds later, they resurface, gulping down their prey. Then, it is back to the air again, to wheel and glide over the deep, almost landlocked, inlet.

The shoal today can't be big, otherwise more birds would be working it. For those that are, it is the day's work to harvest all they can. They industriously soar and dive, time after time, oblivious of my presence. I sit in the sun and watch them. Lazy days.

On the nearby cliffs, the sea thrift is pink, and the scurvy grass is covered in white flowers. Sea campions are in bloom, and primroses and dog violets are everywhere. French gorse is at its most glorious, the dwarf willows are covered in pastel-green catkins and the sycamores in young red leaves. On the verges, road-kill badgers, foxes and mink lie still and bloody, a feature of almost every rural journey we make. Four fat raven chicks sit in their nest above the sea at Coomalacha; they will soon fly. Fledglings are already in the nests of many wild birds, and marauding cats skulk in the lanes, far from home.

*

When we lived in a remote house and fed the dog in the yard, large slugs would come at night and feed on the leavings. On warm nights from late May onward, they would mate. In fact, slugs are hermaphroditic and can fertilise themselves, but mating with a partner must be more enjoyable because this is what they most often do, and each partner lays eggs after mating. They meet on the ground and crawl around in a circle, nose to tail, for up to an hour. Then, one slug climbs the nearest vertical surface, followed closely by the other. At some point favoured by both, they stop and wind around one another. Now, a sticky mucus is exuded. This becomes a strong, silver thread via which, still entwined in their love-knot, they lower themselves from a salient and, hanging head downwards, mate in mid air. After mating, they disentangle. One climbs back up, while the other lowers itself, on a further extension of the thread, to the ground. Within a few weeks, pearly eggs, like sago, are laid by each under logs or stones, later hatching into tiny sluglets. This mating process was witnessed by Anne, a city girl, living in the country, one moonlit night. An artist intrigued with the natural world, she described it as beautiful. I wrote a poem based on her report....

MOLLUSC LOVE

they nightly leave bright trails
along the lane
they eat what dog rejects
wild cats disdain
soft gleaming gobbets gliding to the feast
Anne finds them not disgusting in the least

big slugs entwining is a lovely sight
she once described to me as seen by night
the bodies hanging on a silver thread
as sinuous as molten gouts of lead
turning like sweetbreads
basting in the moon

_ _

SUMMER

It's wonderful that one can still find, just beyond the village houses, a soft and aromatic meadow to collapse into of a warm August evening. The grass is so tall one can see only the sky, blue and cloudless, above. Time stops and rewinds to childhood meadows of long, sweet grass and drowsy evenings when the world stood still.

Above, is a blue infinity. A two-foot-high palisade of seeding grasses, docks, dandelion clocks, hawksbit and tall clovers surrounds one. Dandelion seeds, on their parachutes, drift by. A verse I wrote about a childhood holiday on my uncle's farm in the Golden Vale enters my head. "And time goes by, like drifting down/ On a summer wind, beyond the town...". But here, deep in this nest amongst the grasses, even the small breeze that licks the meadow can't be felt.

The ground between me and the sea below is a speckled carpet of plants and flowers, half of which I can't name or describe. This world - the life of these plants, their opening and closing, sprouting and dying - moves in a reality blithely oblivious of ours. The air is awash with their scent. It reminds me of childhood, coming home from swimming at the end of hot summer days, walking through meadows with clouds of pollen, butterflies and daddy longlegs rising from under our tough bare feet.

A white gull soars in the infinity. The old dog scuffles about and makes a den of her own beside me. Silence returns, broken only by the small sounds of insects going about their business, the stop-go cooing of wood pigeons, the solitary caw of a crow.

At ten at night, as I stroll home, a heron comes down out of the high sky behind me, gliding on wings as capacious as half-umbrellas. Without a single wing beat, it glides and circles. Then, long legs stretching forward, big wings braking and folding, it alights, without a ripple, in the sun-red sea.

As I near the village, I see smoke curling from a chimney - a cold person, perhaps, or maybe it's just the look of the fire that they like. The water in the channel is a sheet of vermilion at the edge of the dark sand. The lights of the seaside street wink softly and the pub beckons, with summer visitors, camaraderie and cheer. Heigh-ho, aren't we the blest ones!, I tell myself. Few places can beat Ireland of a warm summer night!

A poem for Summer

One summer evening, watching the comings and goings of the birds crowded on the sea stacks below the Old Head of Kinsale, I suddenly noticed a peregrine falcon perched under the cliff edge opposite me. Top of the pile, literally and biologically, this small, solitary bird could take any bird it wanted from the metropolis of birds beneath it. Dive, at up to 120 mph, strike, and carry off a fine, fat fulmar; then have supper on the ledge, edged with sea pinks, high over the gin-clear sea.

FALCON

top of the pile she stands
solitary on a ledge
over the metropolis of birds
the high rises and balconies

it's a fine evening for killing
the sun warm on the cliff
the air clear
the sea calm
the tall stacks
thick with dinners

when she flies out
the air stills
when she stoops
the air screams
when she dives
she takes their heads off
her beak is flint
her talons sapphires

small and alone she stands
by a bed of pink sea thrift
she is not pink or thrift
blood red is her colour
killing is her trade

AUTUMN

There is no light like Autumn sunlight for brilliance and clarity. Everything shines. Artists may consider that winter better reveals the truth of colours, but I'm happy with the world gilded by an Autumn sun. Yellows, oranges, russets, reds. Leaves on the trees, and leaves carpeting the forest floor. Green grass sparkling, blue skies and blue sea.

Red admiral butterflies are on the wing, flying as high as the tree tops - butterflies ascending, leaves descending. A robin sings, its red breast bright as a glowing coal amongst the ivy. Red berries on the lacquered holly. A glorious bullfinch on an alder top. I walk through the dappled woods and down onto the green, cliff fields speckled with daisies, the blue Atlantic before us, under a blue sky.

I sit on a stone wall in the warm sun. The only sound is the sea breaking quietly on the rocks, the hum of a bee as it passes, the shrill cry of a sea bird. As the ancient Persian poet Khyam said, approximately,
A loaf of bread beneath the bough,
A flask of wine, a book of verse and thou,
Beside me, singing in the wilderness, is paradise enow.
There's no singer here, no bread or wine or verse, except the half remembered lines and missing stanzas in my memory. There's no "thou", unless that "thou" is a Great Creator responsible for all this, for there isn't a human soul in any direction. As Gerard Manley Hopkins wrote, *"Glory be to God for dappled things...."*

The tide is low and, just beyond the rocks, brown kelp breaks the blue surface, shining like the heads of glossy sea otters I once saw in California.

Our country is so beautiful that I choose it to live in before any other. In two circumscribings of the globe, nowhere I have been can better this West Cork coast on this November morning. As I walk south, the headlands between me and the sun are cut out in black silhouettes. They frame silver bays and inlets dancing in the sun like a million mirrors.

Suddenly, there is a flurry at the sea's edge below me, where the waves break over the kelp. Through binoculars, I watch a gull step ashore with a yellow starfish which it shakes, turns over a few times and then consumes with a gulp. Some gull, some gullet!

It returns to the sea and swims over the kelp, a few feet from the rocks. A cormorant pops up nearby, looking surprised, and then I hear a honk, a very un-gull like, un-cormorant like sound. A hundred yards further out, a grey seal raises its flat, shiny head above the surface. I look away to see how the gull is reacting and when I look back, the seal is gone.

In a field, there are dark green circles and whorls on the grass, where mushrooms grow in rings in August. "They're made by horse's pee!", a little girl recently told me. So much for fairy rings. Science advances and the leprechauns retreat!

Homeward bound, I pass again through the woods and now find long, meandering 'drifts' of Blewits where the wind dispersed the spore in ghostly patterns like sand devils on a beach. A good appetite, and now I have a small feast of blue-leg mushrooms for lunch!

Near home, a flock of godwits in formation is flying over the bay, a flash of white bellies and dark backs as they spin and turn. On the water, close into the beach, an extended family of mergansers, the drakes with black heads and white collars, the ducks with henna-coloured crew-cuts, preen on the still surface. It's two hours since I left the house. I said I'd be away a half an hour, but nature waylaid me. Walking into the yard, I hear a burst of bird song. Can it be? Yes, it is a song thrush, carolling in November!

*

One cold, grey Autumn evening, I saw a neighbour, a well-travelled old man, looking out his window at swallows on the telegraph wires over a beach in West Cork. "What are they doing, all together?" he asked me. "They're gathering, to leave for Africa..." "I'd go with them if I could!" he said.

SIPS AND SWALLOWS

Look out!
The swallows going south
blacken the wires
last posts before the sea

From quiet farms as sun goes out
as yards grow cold
from barns and rafters
the shadows flicker on the fields
summer's rearings darken the meadows

On the wires the old wait
vets of the mile-high club
sharpening cold wings to slice through
latitudes
tread the night skies
on the high trek to south of the sun
or fall for once and all
through the net of stars

The young flutter and dash
flash in first feather
caught in the throng and twitter adventure -

Always, before, I went
migrant of fancy
took flight when the sun dimmed

No more:
the time has come when I can't go
with the will or the winter
too old now -

They used to say but
listen: it's the same everywhere
the daily grub
the airborne lepidoptera

Yes but the weather's better see
the scene new
and that makes all the difference -

Don't tell me caution -
caution? - I'd go on the next wind
with the next flight
tail off over the sea
be spec to twitchers
in cold winter ricks
and I with swallows -

There is no staying and no second chance
the flock moves on
the winds push
the moon beckons
the young dash out
splitting the sky

I loved the swallows of my youth
and the gulps of middle years

now I sip from a small cup
the time's near up
bare wires divide these days going nowhere
fast

_ _

WINTER

Often, these December days, the ebbed bay is dull grey and the golden plover are not golden. Sometimes, in the evenings or mornings, the sunlight breaks through, low and yellow in the sky, and when it catches the flocks, they are suddenly like gold mats on the mudbanks, gold upon slicks of gold, with channels like molten spills in between. From the heights above, the creeks and flats look like an art nouveau brooch, frozen and still until, all at once, the flocks take to the sky.

Five thousand birds as one, they exult in air, sweeping, drifting, dashing, now as an arrow, now as a sickle, now climbing, now hanging, now fluttering back onto the mud like falling leaves.

On Christmas Day, the primrose flowers were yellow - although still furled - in the ruins of the abbey that faces the bay. On Stephen's Day, they opened to the sky. It was an afternoon of lowering clouds, with the weather soft and warm so that after ten minutes walking one shed one's jacket and after another twenty minutes, one's sweater, and ended up carrying half one's wardrobe for most of the walk.

Our route was the wild cliffs, with the sea breaking on jagged rocks below us and mounting in huge, grey swells. The paths we walked were made by foxes or hares; there are no cattle in this terrain, the sheer drops from the cliffs too dangerous and the land eroding more every year.

The sun, when it broke through the clouds, was yellow, turning to red. Towards sunset, its rays spotlighted a derelict house on a headland, miles from its nearest neighbour, making the window, in the westward gable, glow as if there was a Christmas candle inside.

Was it re-inhabited, we joked, had it been squatted by strangers? No, nobody but locals could have found it, and they are all well-housed these days. It had to be the ghosts, we concluded, half-seriously, and the light in the window the same light that struck it on winter evenings when they lived. Often, they must have seen it as we did now, crossing the dark fields and the stones-on-stones that once was a village, on Christmases long past.

As we walked above a deep fissure in the cliff, a chorus of sharp cries sounded out below us, and a troop of choughs rose, black and ghostly, against the cobalt light. Edging closer, I saw where they sheltered on a ledge eighty feet above the sea, the black crevice barely perceptible in the near dark. This would be their nesting place in spring. No four-legged predator could reach them there; only a peregrine or black-backed gull could be a threat.

As the night came down, we crossed rough fields in the near pitch-black, stumbling over whin bushes and sheep. "What is that light in the distance", I asked, "across the fields and the stone walls?" "That," said our friend, smiling, "Is Butlerstown; that is our beacon..."

At the pub in Butlerstown, there was music and song around the fire, friends met by arrangement and teetotal teenage offspring on stand-by to drive us all home. A few pints downed, a few airs aired and bonhomie abroad, with a friend in good voice, unexpectedly back for Christmas from Australia.

On the way home, a fine fox springs from a ditch and in two bounds crosses the road and leaps like a racehorse at full stretch into the ditch opposite. The courage of nature is awesome. A dog would never make such a jump in the darkness of the night with the danger of barbed wire strands, a broken leg, a gashed face, a lost eye.

As we drive on, we pass houses on the road lit up with a thousand bulbs, burning the future for Christmas. I think of the dying sunlight on the window of the ruin, and candles shining out a welcome in lonely windows. Times have changed so fast!

*

Late one winter night, I rose from the TV where I was watching a Dáil debate and, standing in the front garden, found myself in ageless world, under a brilliant moon, listening to the birds out on the mud flats.

TONIGHT IN PARLIAMENT

whooops -
the big moon night! -
space -
crisp as a bark -
light -
you could read the newspaper -

or nip back in
and catch the news
the present crisis -
Tonight in Parliament...

out here
the ebbed estuary
moves under the moon
with the sludge animation of a fast glacier
that's how much goes on

the moon light rubs on leaden pools
and bars
and spits
lagoons and sea wracks

abaft
the beds where mussels lie
watching heaven with a single eye
tonight in parliament

tonight in bars
the mermaids purse
and sand banks sift
and flounders riddle

while out on cockle winking sands
in perma time
the bird tribes
gather

through lunar fog
they hoot and creak
make fearful din
and gunga din
and grunts
and flare-ups

outrageous!
mr speaker....

ten thousand rising cheep and chucks
hear, hear!
here, there
all blessèd night -
in clock stopped time -
Tonight in Parliament

_ _

Damien Enright has been writing a weekly environmental column for the Irish Examiner since 1990. Author of A Place Near Heaven, A Year in West Cork, and eight walking guides to West Cork and Kerry, he has also written and presented a series of heritage programmes for RTE TV. His poetry has been published in Poetry Ireland Review, The Steeple, nth position etc. He lives in West Cork.

In Ireland's mild climate snow is still a rare enough commodity. Here, I photographed our highest mountain, Corrán Tuathail in County Kerry, the day after some light snowfall. By the time I had set up, the snow was melting quickly, exposing the flanks of this beautiful mountain once more.

A male Red Grouse calls from a raised hummock in the heather of the Wicklow Mountains National Park. This behaviour warns rival males that this territory is taken.

Many people will not like this image of a Golden Eagle due to the wing tags and radio tracking ariel on the bird. However, I choose to think of this picture as an image of hope. The tags are of vital importance to the reintroduction of this amazing bird and with luck we will soon see tag-free birds, born in Ireland, soaring over us again.

The crimson berries of the Mountain Ash let us know that summer is at an end and autumn is taking hold.

Orange Peel Fungus growing on the gravel of a woodland path

Although often disliked by gardeners, as they eat many new buds from trees and shrubs, the male Bullfinch is one of our most beautiful birds.

Spending most of their time in the treetops of coniferous forests, the Crossbill will at times come down to drink. Seen at close range, it cannot be confused with any other bird due to its strange crossed mandibles. The male of this species, seen here, is more colourful than the female.

A Redshank is reflected perfectly on a bright, calm morning.

At high tide Black-tailed Godwits fly to a roost where they will wait for the water to recede and uncover their feeding grounds once again.

I have usually photographed Red Deer when they are angry and aggressive during the rut in autumn. For this book I wanted a softer image. This stag was grazing peacefully in the lowland area of Killarney National Park and his antlers were still in the velvet of summer. I waited until he moved into a position in front of the flowering rhododendron and then made the picture.

A Hedge Brown butterfly hangs upside down from a sprig of heather.

I found this Otter fishing in a small lagoon just after sunrise one morning. After a while it went into a gap in the vegetation opposite me and was out of sight for a while. Suddenly it appeared again, framed perfectly by the bright green grasses and looking straight at the camera.

IRELAND'S MAMMALS *by Juanita Browne*

The words 'Irish nature' conjure up a whole host of images, sounds and smells, including:
a treasured glimpse of a pine marten hunting at night on the limestone pavements of the Burren, near Ballyvaughan, in Co. Clare;
a badger lumbering from his sett at nightfall, heading out to search for earthworms under the moonlight in Co. Wicklow;
the sounds of the red deer rutt in Killarney National Park on an autumn evening;
a grassland dotted with bee orchids, spotted orchids, twayblade, and buttercups; the sweet perfume of fragrant orchids filling the senses;
the deafening sounds of harbour seals hauled out at a colony off the coast of Cork;
an urban fox stepping onto a porch in Dublin to finish off the milk left out for a pet cat; while an otter slides down a muddy riverbank in Cavan for a night's fishing. At dusk, a colony of Leisler's bats wake up in a cave roost in Tipperary, and flood out into the night skies. Our countryside is truly alive.

I have been fascinated by animals for as long as I can remember. Big ones, small ones, ones that gallop, crawl, slither, shuffle or hop! It didn't matter. Spiders, frogs, bats and bugs intrigued me. Penguins were a particular favourite on early childhood visits to the zoo. As I grew older it was the lives of mammals that really held my interest, perhaps because we humans are mammals too. So I could relate to the family grouping described in a chimpanzee documentary by Jane Goodall or I could see the intelligence behind the eyes of my dog, Fozzie. I was impressed by the adaptations mammals possessed for survival - the skills that allowed them to find food, make homes, defend themselves and court, and successfully rear young - and how they fitted in with their surroundings and other animals and plants. I also learned about our physiological similarities, for example, the fact that cows, horses, deer, sheep, otters, stoats, hares,

dolphins, whales, badgers and bats feed their young in the same way as human mothers do. I was enthralled by the amazing feats of mammals - for example, that elephant seals can stay submerged underwater for up to two hours and can dive to depths of 1,500 metres. And I was captivated by the diversity of these animals, from the tiny Kitti's hog-nosed bat, which weighs only 1.5g, to the blue whale, the largest animal that has ever lived on earth, weighing over 100 tonnes - 100 million times the weight of the world's smallest mammal. The variety in form in the Class Mammalia produced animals hugely different to each other - such as the elephant, zebra, cheetah, wolf, platypus, narwhal, bear, mole, walrus, armadillo, sloth, and hedgehog. Whatever the reason, I became fascinated by our wild mammals.

There are 4,680 mammal species in the world. A small number of these are found in Ireland - over 20 land mammals, nine bats, two seals and over 20 whale and dolphin species. This small selection of land mammals causes some to consider the Irish fauna uninteresting, trivial or unexciting. But I disagree. We must remember that the Irish mix of flora, fauna, habitats and landscapes is unique and the reasons for our limited biodiversity form interesting stories in themselves. Our ecological history includes such extinct beasts as the giant Irish deer, lemming, arctic fox, reindeer, spotted hyena, brown bear, grey wolf, and woolly mammoth. Our list of extant mammalian inhabitants includes such creatures as the pygmy shrew, weighing in at only 5g, and the red deer at 200kg. Our current combination of wildlife is the result of many factors, including our latitude, isolation from continental Europe and some 9,000 years of habitation by man.
Ireland is a land of varied habitats, a patchwork of farmland, woodland, cliff and marsh, sand dunes, caves, heath, bracken, grassland, bog, fens and flushes, turloughs, lakes, ponds, springs and swamps. We have over 7,800 kilometres of coastline. This island is home to mammals that live in water, such as our

otter; those that make their homes underground, such as the badger, and mammals that can fly - our nine bat species. In June 2001, three killer whales swam up the River Lee and spent the summer in Cork Harbour, reminding us of the magnificent cetaceans found in Irish waters.

We often forget that many of this country's wild animals lived here before man arrived. The red squirrel lived in Ireland since before the last ice age. The Irish stoat has lived here for many thousands of years and has been found to be sufficiently different from stoats elsewhere so as to be considered a unique Irish subspecies. Stoat bones found in a cave in Cork are 35,000 years old. Bones from the Irish mountain hare found in Waterford date back 28,000 years and again it is a subspecies unique to Ireland.
The otter is another of our oldest residents and has been found here for at least 10,000 years. The otter has become extinct in much of Europe due to hunting, habitat destruction and pollution, so there must be an impetus for conserving Ireland's otter population. Though rare in the rest of Europe, Leisler's bat is widespread throughout Ireland - again making the conservation of the Irish population most important.

Humans have always tried to control nature as much as possible, manipulating it to our own ends. We hear 'management' language in agriculture, such as 'meat-growing' or 'increasing milk-yield', which can cause one to forget the living, breathing animals being discussed. One could be forgiven for mistaking it for the language of a factory involved in the production of inanimate products rather than sentient beings. Knowledge of our wildlife and how it lives independently from man reminds us of nature's powers and of a wild animal's resilience in facing the modern world's challenges. The greatest threats to the world's biodiversity today can be explained by the acronym HIPPO, i.e. Habitat Destruction, Invasive Species, Pollution, Population (human over-population) and Overharvesting.

All too often, our countryside and its wildlife is seen as the realm of farmers and hunters, and perhaps of a small number of Latin-speaking scientists. But this shouldn't be the case. Our environment is part of our heritage and as such belongs to us all. Many Irish people have lost a direct connection to the countryside, and children today often know more about exotic species from far-flung places such as Madagascar, through modern media, than they do about the wildlife outside their own doors.

People who are concerned by environmental issues are often perceived as being anti-progress but 'conservation' does not automatically mean halting all development. Nor does it mean that the countryside must be left alone, without man's interference. On the contrary, many of our richest biodiversity areas are a result of traditional management and there are few truly wild places left in this country, so management is often important. Today's conservationists understand the importance of working with businesses, farmers and local communities towards a type of progress that takes best conservation practice into account. There are many small compromises that can be made that can prevent untold damage to wild species and habitats. For example, a roof or bridge renovation that is well planned and enrols the help of a bat specialist and environmental consultant will save time and money in the long term. It is often very simple to maintain an entrance to a traditional bat roost so as not to disturb an important species, while at the same time fulfilling planning obligations and responsibilities under wildlife legislation. Likewise new road schemes should take wildlife habitats and local species into account. Habitat fragmentation is one of the most serious threats to wildlife conservation. Habitats can be fragmented by linear transportation infrastructure, such as roads, railways and canals, and by new land uses.
Europe has the densest network of roads in the world, carving up the countryside into smaller and smaller habitat areas. Many of these roads not only cause wildlife mortality but can also cause a 'barrier effect', preventing the natural dispersal of animals that is so vital to species survival.

In order to understand the threat posed to species conservation by habitat fragmentation one must understand the lifestyle of a species. Many of our wild mammals, such as deer and badgers, must range over large areas to find enough food. The badger lives in family groups in large territories, covering up to 200 hectares. There is usually a main sett, and a number of smaller setts, usually located in woodland areas or under hedgerows. Some setts contain hundreds of metres of tunnels and many chambers for sleeping and rearing young. During nighttime foraging, the badgers use traditional pathways through their territories. If a new road traverses a territory, animals can become cut off from important feeding or breeding grounds. I regularly see dead badgers at the same spot of road on the M7, which must cross one of these traditional foraging paths. A well-positioned underground tunnel could prevent these deaths.

While there has been little research into habitat fragmentation in Ireland, it is known that traffic is the largest cause of badger deaths in Britain, amounting to an estimated 50,000 badgers per year, 100,000 foxes, and 40,000 deer. In Sweden, almost two-thirds of otter mortality is due to road traffic, and in the Netherlands cars kill at least two million birds. 70% of barn owl mortality is caused by traffic accidents.

Careful route planning for new roads can protect Special Areas of Conservation and specially designed green bridges, ecoducts and animal underpasses can help to reconnect fragmented habitats. Alongside our efforts to travel faster on our new roads, we should recognise the existing 'wild commuters' and try to facilitate their safe passage through the countryside. Without careful planning, buildings, roads and conifer plantations could create such a fragmented countryside that our wildlife habitats and corridors are lost forever.

An Ecological Crossroads

Ireland's landscape is changing rapidly. New housing developments, roads, shopping centres and industrial parks are appearing at an astounding rate across the country. Unlike other European countries, such as Germany and the Netherlands, Ireland's environment had escaped the worst effects of industrialisation until relatively recently. Therefore, we still possess some of the best examples of blanket and raised bogs in the world; much of our countryside is still crisscrossed with hedgerows that act as 'arteries' for our wildlife; and our rivers and lakes have remained relatively unpolluted. Ireland is still a safe haven for important species that are endangered or extinct in other parts of Europe. But today we find ourselves at a very important junction in our environmental history. Over the past 30 years, farming practices have intensified; wetlands have been drained and hedgerows have begun to be removed, or are neglected. Habitat destruction, pollution, and the concentrated planting of monocultures pose serious threats to wildlife. Today's planning decisions will impact on the future health of our environment and its wildlife.

In today's busy Ireland it is easy to forsake our natural surroundings and disregard the importance of a healthy environment when compared to quality of living, healthcare, housing, or shortening our commuting time to work. Hence the common belief that there are no 'votes' in environmental issues. If we want to conserve Ireland's natural heritage, we must change this assumption, and make our political representatives sit up and take notice. We must also take responsibility for our own impacts on the environment - we all produce an 'ecological footprint' through our lifestyles which it is our responsibility to minimise. The 'Think Global; Act Local' approach will help preserve the earth's biodiversity. Our wild animals have lived on this island for many thousands of years and are the living barometers of the health of our environment, which ultimately affects us all. The great ecologist Edward O. Wilson warns: "When we destroy ecosystems and extinguish species, we degrade the greatest heritage this planet has to offer and thereby threaten our own existence."

Getting acquainted with our wildlife and Ireland's unique landscape is hugely rewarding. It is a gift you can give your children and one they will cherish for the rest of their lives. It is so enriching to be able to walk along a riverbank and recognise the call of a songbird or trace

the trail of a badger through an open field, or follow the
footsteps of an otter across a sandy beach at dawn.
Let not the roar of the Celtic Tiger be the only wild
sound our children recognise.

Juanita Browne studied Zoology at Trinity College
Dublin and is an editor and writer. She recently
published 'Ireland's Mammals', a wildlife book for all
ages. (ISBN 0-9550594-0-2). Please see
www.irishwildlife.ie for more information. Tel. 00353 (0)
86-3442140

Foxes are becoming common in urban areas these days but I still prefer to photograph them in rural settings. Watching cubs in the spring is one of my favourite things.

By late summer a mature woodland is a carpet of green. I made this image just after a heavy shower which gave a freshness to the leaves.

The future of the forest.

The Sparrowhawk
is our most
common bird of
prey in Ireland. It is
superbly agile in
flight, making it a
formidable hunter
of other birds.
Here an adult
feeds the hungry
chicks with its
latest victim.

Found from late summer and through the autumn, the Fly Agaric is an easy fungi to recognise. This beautiful specimen was photographed in Glengarra woods in County Tipperary.

At first glance this may look like the coat of a fury, colourful mammal but it is in fact the body of a Convolvulus Hawkmoth. This extremely large moth migrates to Ireland in small numbers during the summer. This specimen was found in a greenhouse but died soon after it was found.

Having seen Jays visit a local garden trying to get some peanuts from the feeders, I put a handful of nuts down on the lawn nearby and waited. This bird soon arrived and didn't leave until it had all the nuts in its crop.

As evening falls, Lesser Horseshoe Bats will fly in and out of the exit to their daytime roost to check if it is dark enough to start hunting. This bat was "light sampling" in such a way when I made this image.

The delicate Long-tailed Tit doesn't often stay still for very long as it flits around the trees and hedges.

Not liked by many, the Rook is a powerfully built bird which can look very aristocratic when it strikes a certain pose.

Damp mornings are great for seeing Snails. This one was slithering around on a moss covered wall when I came across it, and I liked the combination of muted colours.

Often found in woodlands, the Bugle can be easy to miss but on close inspection is quite a beautiful plant.

A Common Earth-ball fungi pushes through a patch of moss.

(right) *This little house had been built to to feed small garden birds and to keep magpies and rooks away from the nuts. The entrance hole however had been made a little too big and the local Red Squirrels found it a great place to stop for a bite.*

(left) *A Pintail on a winter morning.*
(below) *Blackbird heaven.*

(above) *The back of a grain store is a perfect place to find a Brambling in Winter.*
(below) *Water droplets fall from the bill of a Whooper Swan as it takes a drink.*

(overleaf) *Ice patterns on a frozen lake shore.*

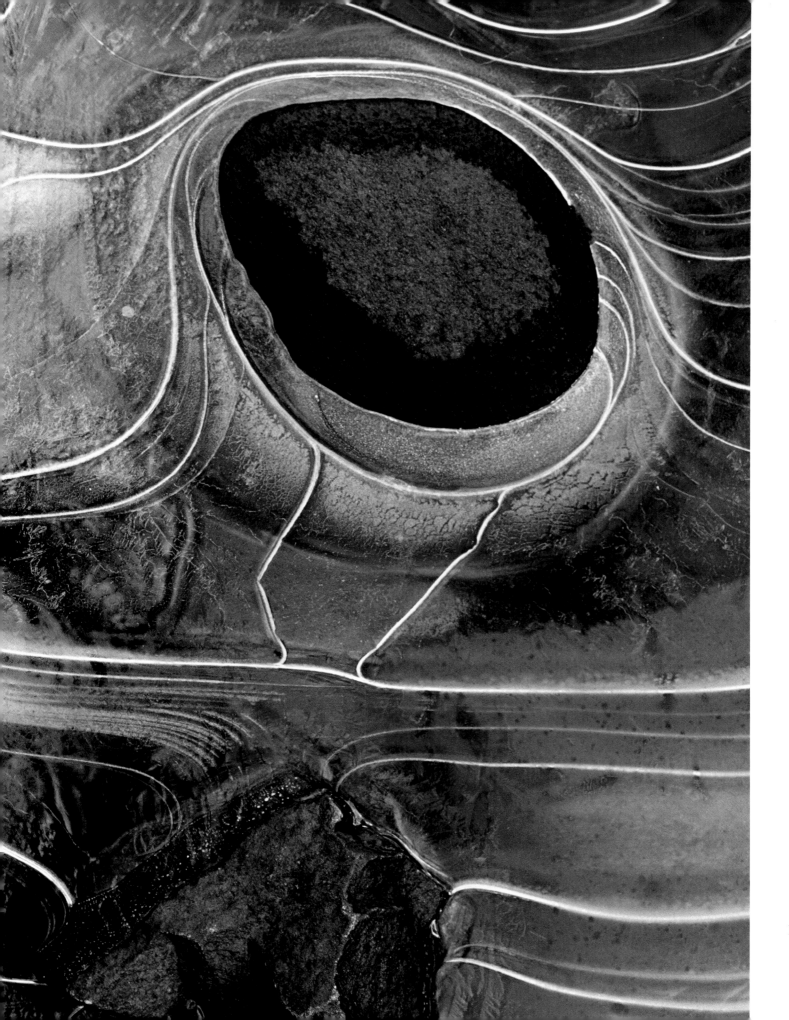

WHALES AND DOLPHINS IN IRISH WATERS *by Pádraig Whooley*

Background

The Irish wildlife enthusiast faces certain insurmountable challenges in observing truly native Irish mega fauna. If fortunate enough to witness the outstretched wings of a golden eagle gliding the thermals, it is most likely that the egg came from a nest in the Scottish highlands and was artificially incubated and hand-reared by researchers. Our largest land predator, the fox, is little bigger than a domestic cat; while the urban fox population, scavenging on garbage, appears to be faring better than its country cousins. Our native grazers, the red deer are now confined to a few small pockets and are under intense pressure from both Norman invaders and cheap Japanese imports.

When most people think of Ireland and its wildlife, they do not readily make the association with our Island nation and its nutrient-rich waters, which are home to almost one-third of the 84 cetacean species (whales, dolphins and porpoises) known to science. This is a mistake; but the perception is changing fast, as a growing army of wildlife enthusiasts are becoming aware of Ireland's best kept wildlife secret and focusing their attention and optics on Ireland's waters, home to Europe's first whale and dolphin sanctuary.

Irish waters are, at least seasonally, home to an impressive diversity of whales and dolphins. In fact if you include our two pinniped species, the grey and common seals, our marine mammals comprise almost 50% of Ireland's mammalian fauna. Of these, cetaceans are the largest group, both in terms of the numbers of species and sheer size. To date, 24 species have been recorded in Irish waters, ranging from the tiny harbour porpoise to the giant blue whale, and from coastal species like the frequently seen bottlenose dolphin to the rarely seen beaked whales that live in deep offshore habitats. Added to this is the potential to witness marine non-mammal species, such as the world's second largest fish, the basking shark, or vagrant marine reptiles such as the leatherback turtle, or perhaps a glimpse of a summer visitor, like the sunfish.

Basic Ecology

Cetaceans break down into two subgroups, the toothed whales or *odontocetes*, which have teeth, and the larger baleen whales or *mysticetes*, which instead of teeth have modified hair-like structures, called baleen plates, which act as a giant sieve. As a rule of thumb, the smaller cetaceans such as the porpoises and dolphins have teeth. The obvious exception to this is the Sperm whale of *Moby Dick* fame, which has an impressive array of teeth on the lower jaw, designed for feeding on deep-water squid. The toothed whales comprise 75% of Irish cetacean species. The remainder are the large baleen whales, of which the minke whale is the most frequently observed in all Irish waters.

Ireland's high cetacean species diversity, suggests that our seas are in relatively healthy condition in terms of water quality and prey abundance and that they offer suitable habitats for toothed and baleen whales alike. So while islands generally sustain a lower diversity of both land animals and birds, the opposite can be said of our marine mammals who live along our rocky shoreline, in our estuaries, bays, shallow inshore and deep offshore habitats.

How can you become involved?

Whether you've just a passing interest or are a keen wildlife observer, everyone can contribute to cetacean conservation. One of the best ways of doing this is by reporting your observations, although we do appreciate that identifying cetaceans is not always an easy task, as sightings are typically brief and distant. But as with most types of wildlife watching, the more often you do it, the better you get at it, and there is surely no better time to become actively involved in recording cetaceans in Irish waters.

When to whale watch?

Whale watching is best carried out during settled weather, when seas are calm, winds are light and visibility is clear. Early mornings and late afternoons may bring best light conditions, but don't let this deter you from watching at other times of the day, as whales and dolphins don't keep a schedule. The more flexible you can be with your time, the more likely you are to maximise your time watching in suitable sea conditions. Don't assume that the best weather will be during the summer months, as heat haze and sea fog can so easily scupper your attempts to go whale watching during periods of warm weather. Winter time can just as easily bring settled weather, with cold, crisp but clear Arctic air, which allows perfect visibility out to the distant horizon.

Where to whale watch?

Although cetaceans can in theory turn up anywhere, as has in been evidenced recent years by Killer whales in the River Lee, and a sei whale in Larne Lough, the best places for land-based whale watching in Ireland are elevated sites such as headlands and cliff-tops and of course our offshore islands. We are indeed fortunate that much of our Celtic Sea and Atlantic coastline is fringed by dramatic cliffs and headlands, many of which offer wonderful whale watching potential. These Atlantic promontories jut out into deeper waters, which in effect brings whales and dolphins closer to your vantage point.

Remember, these are potentially dangerous places, so take care and inform people where you are going and when you expect to return, and seek permission from the land owners if the land is privately owned.

How to whale watch?

The more time you spend whale-watching, the better you will get at reading the subtle cues that indicate the presence of whales and dolphins.

These may be:
Circling or diving gannets which frequently reveal feeding porpoises, dolphins or whales, as they drive small fish to the surface when feeding.

Surface disturbances or peculiar looking waves caused by dolphins travelling close to the surface, or a breaching animal.

A brief glint or a sudden reflection on a sunny day may be sunlight catching the water as it runs off the back of a surfaced cetacean.

Temporary vapour plumes or 'blows' hanging on the horizon in windless conditions will likely reveal the presence of either fin or humpback whales which have surfaced.

Optics

The results of a whale watch will be greatly influenced by the type and quality of optics used. A good pair of binoculars will be your minimum requirement, but even these may limit your sightings to harbour porpoises and occasional dolphins that occur inshore. If you want to observe the large aggregations of pelagic dolphins, such as common dolphins, or baleen whales like the fin or humpback whale which often occur further offshore at distances of greater than five miles, you may need to use a spotting scope, mounted on a steady tripod.

The early days of whale watching ….

Everyone will be familiar with Fungie who has enthralled over a million tourists and dolphin enthusiasts, since arriving in Dingle harbour back in 1984. This solitary bottlenose dolphin has over the past 21 years broken all records held by sociable dolphins around the world. But by the 1990s the word was out that Fungie wasn't the only dolphin in Irish waters and commercial dolphin watching, based on a seasonally resident population of over 100 bottlenose dolphins, developed just 50 miles up the coast in the Shannon Estuary. Now there are professional dolphin watching operations based in Kilrush and Carrigaholt, Co. Clare.

Today, there are even greater opportunities to see whales and dolphins as commercial whale watching is now firmly established in West Cork and is beginning to take hold in coastal communities along the south coast. Although such activities will never replace the once great fishing industry that thrived in these waters, whale watching and other such marine tourism products could potentially bring in badly needed revenue to coastal communities reeling from the demise of fishing.

Whale watching In Ireland today……a world of discovery awaits you

I'm frequently asked, where are the best places in the world to go whale watching? My answer has changed considerably over the years. In the early days I'm ashamed to say I may have given quite poor advice, as my reply would have included such exotic locations as British Columbia; Baja, California; or Patagonia. Yes, these are stunning locations, and may offer great whale watching opportunities at certain times of year, but I challenge anyone to produce as consistently high encounter rates of a similarly high species diversity, over as much of the year, as can be observed in Irish waters and in particular those of the south coast.

Since moving to Cork in 1999 I've spent much of my time whale watching from such beautiful locations as the Old Head of Kinsale, Galley Head, and Cape Clear Island. And over these years, I have made the same mistake, by giving an answer when asked that same question…where's the best place to go whale watching? My adjusted answer was of course based on the best information available at the time, which suggested that West Cork was the best place to go whale watching in Ireland. And it may well have been part of the answer, but it was far from the complete picture.

Six years of regular 'timed watches' from West Cork headlands produced encounter rates which compare favourably with some of the best land-based whale watching anywhere on the world's whale watching circuit. Among these were a tally of seven cetacean species from both the Old Head of Kinsale and Galley Head in West Cork. These were: harbour porpoise, common dolphin, bottlenose dolphin, Risso's dolphin, minke whale, fin whale and humpback whale. During the autumn to winter peak in sightings, 90-minute watches would frequently produce sightings of 2-5 species. 100% encounter rates of >1 sighting were achieved for nine months of every year. All this combined with strong inter-annual trends, showing fin and humpback whales arriving each summer and leaving in late winter, often in the company of impressive numbers of common dolphins as they collectively follow the herring shoals inshore.

More recent photo identification studies carried out by the IWDG have shown re-sightings of fin whales that are returning, and of individuals that were photographed frequently enough in the six-month period between summer and winter to suggest that at least some individuals are arriving along our south coast and staying for prolonged periods. So it does indeed look like our waters offer these leviathans a lot more than a brief staging post.

One of the best illustrations of the importance of Irish waters to these giants is the annual return of a humpback whale to West Cork's inshore waters around Galley Head each year in late August. Using photo ID images of distinguishing features on his dorsal fin and tail-fluke, we can confirm that this whale, known locally as "Boomerang", has now returned to the same area in each of the past five years. On four of these years he has retuned within the same 72 hour period. Such re-sighting trends rule out these being mere chance encounters. It is now clear that these waters provide important habitat for this individual humpback whale and at least five other humpbacks which have been catalogued in these waters.

The significance of these encounters can not be understated and should be looked at in the context of the humpback whale designation on the IUCN Red List as "vulnerable". So we are indeed privileged to be able to observe these animals with relative ease off our south coast, and it is incumbent on us to ensure that they are given every opportunity to return in increasing numbers to our waters. They've been absent for long enough.

Since 2003, considerable resources have been spent delivering talks, training workshops and courses on whale observation, recording and species identification. The aim was to raise awareness and to encourage greater reporting from all coastal waters, but targeting those areas in particular where cetacean recording was historically quite low.

The results from this initiative have been very interesting, and indicate, yet again, that my advice on whale watching may not have been quite accurate. It became clear that when people were interested enough to put in the effort watching from their own local headlands, the results were often no less impressive than those encountered along the south coast's "hotspots". It now appears that West Cork has no monopoly on these large whales, and other sites such as Hook Head, Co. Wexford; Ardmore Head, Co. Waterford; and Slea Head, Co. Kerry, are producing equally impressive whale and dolphin encounters throughout much of the year.

We now receive regular reports of cetacean activity from many coastal areas where few were previously reported. And as more and more wildlife enthusiasts catch the whale watching bug, our understanding of these magnificent mammals and our ability to protect them and their habitats improves. So my answer to anyone who asks me that same question today: "where is the best place to see whales and dolphins?", is "somewhere a lot closer to your own doorstep than you might think".

I recall many early morning winter watches, sitting up

on West Cork's cliffs, with nothing but countless miles of ocean in front of me. The excitement of simply not knowing what might pass along my horizon was palpable. Small or large, near or distant, few or numerous, common or rare; you learn to expect the unexpected. I've always described whale watching in Ireland as being like a bag of pick and mix..... you never know what you're going to get.

In many years of whale watching from our headlands I can count on one hand the numbers of times I've felt anything but privileged and inspired after a watch. As long as you're watching in suitable conditions, there will nearly always be something fascinating to catch the eye. It may be a harbour porpoise behaving unusually, or the spectacle of large numbers of common dolphins passing with great energy and speed, attracting hundreds of diving gannets. But I will never forget my early winter encounters with fin whales from the Old Head of Kinsale, when I first observed common dolphins and whales feeding together. Scarcely believing my eyes when a group of eight dolphins peeled off from the main feeding frenzy to bow-ride, four abreast, on each side of the whale's massive head, at it pushed a pressure wave forward. Such opportunities are there for all of us to enjoy, and are without question one of the best wildlife shows in town. And the good news is that the front row seats are absolutely free.

The opportunity for people to enjoy whales and dolphins in Ireland has never been greater. We hope this will encourage you to blow the dust off your binoculars and to sit out on a local headland for a few hours and give it a try. It may introduce you to a whole new area of endeavour. There is very little in natural history that can inspire quite like that first sighting of a breaching whale or close encounter with a pod of dolphins.

We hope you enjoy your whale watch and let us know what you've seen.

Please report your sightings to IWDG:

On-line via the IWDG website www.iwdg.ie sighting section
By emailing full details: date, time, location, species (if known), group size, behaviour, with relevant field-notes and photographs to sightings@iwdg.ie
Enquiries to enquires@iwdg.ie" enquires@iwdg.ie

For more information on dolphin watching in the Shannon visit www.shannondolphins.ie or visit the Shannon Dolphin & Wildlife Foundation centre in Kilrush, Co. Clare.

Pádraig Whooley is Sightings Co-ordinator of the Irish Whale and dolphin Group and has been monitoring cetaceans off the Irish coast since 1999. He is currently conducting photo identification research of fin and humpback whales off the Cork coast. When not watching from the cliff tops, he is promoting Ireland's wealth of cetacean diversity and has written extensively on the subject.

The Basking shark is the biggest fish you can see in Irish waters and although it may look a little scary it is completely harmless to humans.

There are always squabbles and quarrels going on in a Kittiwake breeding colony. With their snow white heads, yellow bills and red mouths they are a striking bird in close-up.

(right) This pair of Great Black-backed Gulls were standing guard over their young which were just on the other side of this rock. These birds are very large and will vigourously defend their nest if you were to stray too close.

A pair of Roseate Terns prepares to copulate at their colony on Rockabill lighthouse station, off the east coast of Ireland. These birds are the rarest of Ireland's breeding terns.

(left) Finding shells on the shoreline is often easy but getting down on your hands and knees can reveal special treasures. These two tiny shells were the brightest I found on a beach of coarse sand. To give you an idea of scale, the lower one was just three millimetres long.

This Fin Whale surfaced so close to our boat that it allowed me to get a close up image of it. These wales are the second largest animal on earth and to see one is a special thrill. At close quarters like this it is simply awe inspiring.

The coastline of Ireland is transformed during summertime by the soft pink of Thrift on the rocks and shoreline.

The constant motion of the tide softens the edges of the shingle until each stone is silky smooth.

A flock of Golden Plovers takes fright - perhaps a peregrine flacon is about - and they all rise simultaneously. As this is a regular occurrence I had decided to try to record this event in an abstract way. I locked the camera in position and set a slow shutter speed to show the movement of the birds as they took off. An alarm call sounded and I released the shutter.

A Greenshank looks alert as it tries to work out what the strange clicking sound is nearby.

Seeing one Humpback Whale up close is very special, seeing two within fifteen or twenty metres of you is truly wonderful. The nearer whale was slapping the water as some sort of communication, while the further one was just lolling on the surface.

I was watching this Grey Heron fishing on an estuary when it caught a large Eel. It had a few problems getting it down as the sequence shows.

The shapes of this dry seaweed echo the waves that brought it to its resting place.

AT THE EDGE OF THE TIDE

by Michael Viney

The length of Ireland's coastline must now, I suppose, be nearing some kind of exactitude, as Earth is scanned obsessively by robots in the sky. But everything depends on where you pace it, and at what moment. Tide lifts and falls; foam reaches up to lick one's boots or curl around a rock. For the beachcomber, the boundary of land and ocean is more a state of mind than any line drawn in the sand. I have been walking the tide line, on and off, for much of my life, each visit a reminder that Earth is very big and I am, in its cosmos, very small: a good working basis for any relationship with nature.

The town where I was young (Brighton, on the English Channel) had a shingle beach, seasonally overlaid with thousands of striped towels and prostrate bodies. But in winter, with the stones washed clean and gleaming, it was possible to step back into the Victorian passion for pebble-collecting. A small, old-fashioned shop off the seafront dazzled me with semi-precious lapidary art: carved and polished onyx, jasper, agate, chalcedony, citrine, carnelian, amethyst - such mystical, ravishing names, and their glowing beauty, implicitly, the gift of the sea. Crunching along beside the waves, I made my choice from the millions of potential gems, and, emptying them out at home, tried to lick them back to life. Nothing in my education matched our pebble beaches to the story of the Earth, but in the crashing of breakers, the hiss of rolling stones, I did make some connection with the planetary world.

Ireland, too, has pebble strands, from the great storm-beaches of the west, terraced with bleached grey ostrich-eggs of limestone and quartz, to the gentler ridges of the south-east, their pebbles sifted and polished from the debris of ancient glaciers (among them, blood-red jaspers swept down the Irish Sea from the granites of Wicklow and Down). There are agates in the old red sandstone quarried by the waves at the tips of Cork and Kerry headlands; amethyst, still, in the quartzite of Achill; aquamarine in the granite of the Mournes. But, living now above a strand in south-west Mayo, my windowsills are crowded with the different flotsam and jetsam of a sandy shore: sea-urchins, crab shells, bird skulls, the vertebrae of dolphins, their curves instinct with the energy of other lives.

The two kilometres of Thallabawn strand lie open to the Atlantic swells just north of the fiord of Killary Harbour, remote enough from human disturbance to let the otter commute between the waves and the little lakes behind the dunes. Most of the sand is made of shells ground small, so that three-spot cowries, like rolled-up finger-prints, stand out in their wholeness in a shattered mosaic ('the dry shells, the toe- and fingernail parings of the sea' in Michael Longley's image). The tiny fragments are blown across the dunes and rain down onto the flat, grassy machair beyond. Here, their calcium is magically recycled into the shells of abundant land snails, some striped in bright yellows and browns and others the big, dark snails that gardeners know. In winter, long lines of these are wedged into the leeward cracks of driftwood fence-posts in the dunes, their shells sand-blasted to delicate shades of blue; on particular moist summer mornings on the other hand, they are all abroad at ground level, silvering the mosses in a reproductive orgy.

Rachel Carson, a marine biologist now better remembered for blowing the whistle on pesticides than for her revelatory books about the sea, once tried to buy the only specimen of the lovely, ocean-drifting violet snail *Janthina* in a shell shop in North Carolina. Rebuffed, she waited on luck, and 'later I found an empty shell, light as thistledown, resting in a depression in the coral rock of Key Largo, where some gentle tide had laid it.' Reading this, I knew her joy, having come upon two of these beautiful, translucent shells, resting within a pace of each other on the tide line. It was a privilege all of a piece with *Janthina's* random lifestyle, since this mollusc travels the surface of the ocean hanging upside down (as we would see it) from a silvery raft made by trapping the wind in bubbles of mucus. It lives on the chance of colliding with, and eating, a little blue jellyfish called *Velella*, or by-the-wind sailor. Sometimes cast up by the million on Ireland's Atlantic shores, this, too, is an ocean drifter, propelled by a little rainbow-coloured sail that it hoists to catch the wind. The odds against snail and jellyfish colliding on the open ocean seem enormous, yet they do this with sufficient frequency to be bonded as predator and prey. When by-the-wind sailors drift ashore, *Janthina* occasionally arrives with them, but snail and jellyfish first meet, far out on the ocean, by bobbing blindly against each other, like toy boats on a park pond.

Infinite chance, infinite time: part of one's pact with the rest of nature is accepting a scale of events quite at odds with our own pell-mell progress. It is a couple of decades since two notable storms, tail-ends of hurricanes, left our strand littered, end to end, with hundreds of washed-up fish. Most were the species from rocky ground out towards the islands - muscular congers, tiny cuckoo wrasse like drifts of pink goldfish, black tadpole fish that no one ever sees. Others we gathered for the freezer: ling, hake, and pollack. A scientist friend, a marine biologist, theorised that they had drowned from the shock of sudden change in temperature as masses of water were overturned offshore. Perhaps, but it has never happened since, in any other storm. But a couple of decades is scarcely a flicker on nature's millennial meter, and words like 'often' or 'rarely' are purely human calibrations. Rarity itself is so often merely a measure of who's around to see.

The more extraordinary events along the shore were once received as part of nature's ordinary chaos, the result of cyclic plagues, random storms, and so on. Today, they are not only more likely to be recorded, but scrutinised for hints of human impact, climate change

and altered patterns in the ocean. We no longer feel sure that what we are watching is 'natural', and mass strandings and mortalities become runes to be read for the future of the planet. What was to be made of a great winter arrival of cuttle-bones (those oval, chalk-white buoyancy aids at the heart of the squid's inshore cousins)? I had seen very few since my English Channel childhood, yet in 1996 came thousands, swept along the south coast and up the west of Ireland. Two winters later, it was little amber-coloured jellyfish, a pelagic ocean drifter, luminous by night (hence its name, Pelagia noctiluca). Arriving by the million, and in every size, it left some beaches glazed in marmalade from Clare to Donegal. The trigger fish of warm waters used to be rare this far north, but a neighbour found seven at once in one of his lobster pots. A vertically-swimming fish with thick lips and sharp teeth, it has every appearance of toughness (and can lock and unlock two dorsal spines to resist being dragged from its hole in a reef), but is not yet suited to survive the Irish winter: one I found washed up on a frosty morning in November was typical of those stranded in the autumn.

It's in winter that I go beachcombing most hopefully, sure that a solitary trudge beside the waves must deserve some unusual reward. Wind lifts the sand in long, pale skeins that hiss around my ankles, and leaves flat stones and shells balanced on little mushroom pedestals. Some distant skeins resolve into flocks of sanderling, dunlin or little ringed plovers: miniature waders stirring ahead of me, swirling about, and settling intently in my wake. Turnstones shuffle seaweed in the long, black scribble of the tide line.

Among the weed, abundant plastic, much of it cosmopolitan: French fish-boxes, Canadian milk-crates, Spanish trawlerballs, American lightsticks (fluorescing lures attracting tuna or squid to the baits of long-line hooks). The long-distance items come hairy with hydroids, minuscule animals dressed as ferny plants, or sprout clusters of goose barnacles, nodding on rubbery necks. They all smell intensely of the sea, a dark-green odour whose chemistry shapes the clouds - and is thus one of the planet's primal fragrances.

At the furthest reach of the tide, along with the lightsticks, lightbulbs, arms and legs of baby dolls, ubiquitous polypropylene pellets, settles a sparse harvest of tropical drift fruits and seeds - the 'sea beans' treasured by generations of beachcombers. Botanically, these are 'peregrine disseminules' of jungle vines and bushes. Their arrival on European coasts has been discussed for at least four centuries: the first Irish record of *Entada gigas*, the prominent and robust 'sea bean', dates to 1696. "It is very easie to conceive," wrote Hans Sloane, the Irish-born founder of the Chelsea Botanic Garden, "that growing in Jamaica in the woods, they may fall from the Trees into the Rivers, or by any other way conveyed by them into the Sea." He posited a westerly trade wind "for at least two parts of three of the Whole Year, so that the Beans being brought North by the Currents from the Gulf of Florida, are put into these Westerly Winds way and may be supported by this means at last to arrive in [Ireland and] Scotland." Sloane's theory, written when the currents of the oceans were scarcely understood, is strikingly accurate. Perhaps a score of species of tropical plants have seeds capable of staying afloat in salt water for about 14 months, the least time it takes a small object to drift across to Europe.

I enjoy digging out things like this, and feeling some connection, however spurious, to past centuries of grand conjecture. It is the sort of thinking that seems right for standing at the sea's edge, gazing west across the breakers. 'Taking an interest in nature' is, or should be, a constant weave of the sensual reaction of the moment and a prompting to find out more. John Fowles, an ardent ambassador for nature between writing his novels, worried that people were too ready to accept a relationship dictated more by science and the act of collection than instinctual emotion and poetry. "We have quite enough facts now," or so he argued. But for me, the moment's feeling is the door to curiosity.

Can one often feel wonder about so much on the shore that is dead (and sometimes very smelly)? In successive winters, years ago, I came upon the eighth and ninth specimens ever found in the world of True's Wonderful Beaked Whale, *Mesoplodon mirus*, rarest of the smaller whales that hunt squid in the deep Atlantic. It was a bumper demonstration of chance, made all the more absurd by hinging on the exact conformation of the animals' two front teeth. This had to be verified, of course, by distant scientific authority, but I was stepping in the sandy footsteps of Frederick William True, an American mammalogist who came upon his prize on a shoal in north Carolina in 1912, and named it 'wonderful' in Latin. Nothing so museum-worthy has drifted my way since then, for all my forensic attendance at cetacean remains. Ireland's first *Architeuthis* would be nice: the spectacular giant squid of deep ocean, with tentacles metres long and eyes the size of dinner-plates.

The beachcombing naturalist carries two visions of the world in his or her head, matching mortuary detail to vigorous images of life. In winter, like the fox, and often in its close-stitched footsteps, I wander from one dead seabird to the next, lingering perhaps at one so immaculate and pristine it seems to have closed its eyes the moment before. Where else can I see how the brilliant beak of a puffin grips a whole feed of sandeels for its young, or spread the huge wing of a gannet to feel how it gathers the air? Even the kelp that litters the strand carries in its glistening curlicues the swirl and flow of the undersea forest, the messages sent throbbing landwards twice a day.

Michael Viney is the author of Ireland: A Smithsonian Natural History and A Year's Turning, both published in Ireland by Blackstaff Press. His weekly column on ecology and the countryside, Another Life, has appeared in The Irish Times since 1977. He lives with his wife Ethna on the coast of County Mayo.

Limpets cling to the rocks as the tides falls and the sun disappears for the night.

I love to see the detail in a bird's feathers when they are at full stretch. This Herring Gull was patrolling the shores of Great Saltee island in County Wexford looking for an easy meal when I made this image.

*Everybody's favourite member of the crow family, the Chough
cannot be confused with anything else due to its bright red bill.*

The Sheep's Bit is common in the countryside but is quite small and is often overlooked. However, its vivid colour and interesting design make it worth looking for.

The Marsh Helleborine is, in my opinion, one of the most striking flowers we have in Ireland.

Perfection. An Early Marsh Orchid sits alone in a sea of green.

(left) *Having caught a small fish and collected some weed in its bill in the process, this Great Crested Grebe takes its prey to its waiting young.*

Where it is found, the Bloody Crane's-bill can be very abundant and it is a noted plant of the Burren, where it is dotted all over the landscape during the summer. I chose to close-in on the flower head for this portrait to show its vivid colour.

A Small Heath butterfly alights for a moment on a plantain.

The Hen Harrier is one of my favourite birds. A formidable hunter, they are poetry in motion when in flight. If you look closely at this female you will notice a tiny set of legs hanging below her. Not hers, but those of her prey, most probably a Meadow Pipit, clutched tight in her own talons as she returns to her hungry brood. A truly magnificent sight.

Looking north over a woodland, I set my camera to expose the night sky for an extended period of time. As the Earth turns on its axis, the stars appear to revolve around Polaris - the North Star. Seeing the universe like this, it seems that we and our co-inhabitants on this planet are just a very small part of a big picture.

153

Photographic Notes

I regularly do talks and slide shows for groups and clubs around the country and I am often asked about the cameras and accessories that I use. For those readers who have an interest in the technical side of my work I have given details here of the equipment I use and the reasons why, as well as some notes and observations on the way I work.

From film to digital

For the last few years, the question which has always been asked whenever photographers gathered was "Are you shooting digital yet?". Many people left film behind quite early on in the digital revolution but because of the speed of development of digital cameras and accessories some may have regretted moving so fast. Almost every month the major camera manufacturers announced a new model which was better, had more pixels and downloaded them faster than the last one. Each new model was better value than the last and digital cameras are now far cheaper than they were at the end of the 1990's and more importantly, far better.

At the beginning I was sceptical. Having worked as a press photographer when the first generation of digital camera bodies were starting to be used by professionals I had seen some of the early models in action. What I saw was that they were cumbersome, slow to use and produced very low quality images which were really only for use in the newspaper industry. When things started to improve I watched the progress in camera development and read all the reports on each new camera as it appeared on the market. Only when I felt fully satisfied that digital would produce images which were of the same or better quality than the high quality slide film I was using did I make the move. Being a Canon user with a large collection of lenses and accessories which I loved, it had to be a Canon camera.

And so in 2004 I purchased the Canon EOS 1Ds. This camera has a full frame sensor and so each of my lenses behaved exactly like they did on my film cameras. With images of over 11 million pixels the quality is excellent and overall I am incredibly happy with it. It has of course now been superseded by the 1Ds Mark 2, which has more pixels and has been improved slightly in other ways but I am still using the 1Ds quite happily. However, I did miss the speed of my old film cameras, which had motor drives capable of six frames per second or so. Very useful when the action is fast and furious. So when the EOS 1D Mark 2 came onto the market with an eight frames per second motor drive and an image size of over 8 megapixels, I couldn't resist the temptation! I'm so glad that I didn't as it is a superb camera. It has a smaller sensor than 35 mm film so there is a multiplication factor with all my lenses but to be honest this can be very useful when needing to get close to some of my more wary subjects. Manufacturers are still improving their products at an astonishing rate but I am glad I made the move to digital when I did, although I will probably wait a while yet before I trade up to the next big thing. With these two camera bodies I feel I have the best of both worlds. One is a full frame camera with a high pixel count, the other one a speed machine with a good sized image and a small multiplication factor. All of the images in this book bar three or four which I

things like "sure we'll just shoot away and fix it up on the computer afterwards", this is simply bad practice and is regularly very noticeable in the final print. When we were all using film - and particularly those of us using slide film - we had to take care of exposure, lighting and composition. Working digitally we should still take the same care in my opinion. I would not consider myself an expert at digital processing but I do try to stick to good practice when dealing with an image.

Finally, and I say this to all those who ask me if they should change from film to digital, there are positive and negative aspects to changing to digital. I would have to say that I could edit a batch of slides from a shoot into a selection of brilliant, good, poor and downright bad far quicker that I can do it with digital images. With a light box and a loupe I could get through a few rolls of film very quickly and bin the rubbish and pick out the best in a few

chose to shoot on film [see note later], were originated on these two cameras and I am happy that the quality is every bit as good and in some cases possibly better than I would have achieved on film.

Having said all that, there are a few other issues to be addressed with digital. Making the image in the camera is just one step of the process and all digital images, just like all scans from film, need a certain amount of work. Knowing how to do this is something that should be learned properly to make the most of digital photography. I have seen some otherwise excellent images ruined by bad digital editing. By the same token I also hear too many photographers saying

minutes. With digital I can see the complete rubbish from a thumbnail size image all right but anything I want to check for critical sharpness etc. must be seen at a bigger size. Then I have to go through the various facets of digital editing with the ones I keep. This all takes time at the computer and if you are like me time is a valuable commodity. I want to be a photographer not a computer operator and there's only so much time in the day. There are also a lot of hidden cost with digital. Apart from the cameras, which are still far more expensive than their film counterparts, we now need a good computer, software for editing and digital storage for both the camera and the computer. The only thing I can say about this is that if you shoot lots of images then you will get your money back quickly enough by going digital but if you only shoot a handful of rolls a year, then digital will be a high cost and may not be worth it.

So why use film? One or two of the images were shot before I moved to digital but that is not the full story. I have retained one of my film cameras for one purpose - long exposures. To make an image on a digital sensor, an electric current is passed across it. For long exposures this continuous current causes distortion in the image that we see as "noise". When the noise reduction facility is used, the camera makes a second exposure after the original one has finished. As far as I know [and this is how it has been explained to me so forgive me if I'm incorrect], the second exposure is just black and is overlaid onto the first image to attempt to reduce noise. For the image of the star trails [pages 152/153] I used an exposure of about two hours. In this case the camera would have been recording for a period of four hours or so. As images of even a few minutes can show a good degree of noise, I chose to shoot on film instead.

Lenses

The lenses I used for this book were just about the same as I have used for the last six or seven years with a few exceptions. Zooms of 17-35mm, 24-70mm and 70-200mm cover the shorter focal lengths. I used to use a 300mm F2.8 but I have actually changed it for a 300mm F4. The reason for this is that this is the lens I use mostly for hand held flight shots and I find the F2.8 version just too heavy for that. On the 1D MK2 body this lens equates to approximately 390mm on a full frame camera and it retains its F4 aperture, which in good light allows plenty of light for good results. At the extreme telephoto end I still use my 600mm F4 lens. Many photographers are now opting for the 500mm F4 lenses as they are a good deal lighter than the 600mm and they are also cheaper. I however wouldn't give up the 600mm for love nor money for extra bit it gives me in terms of pulling power and since it is always used on a tripod the weight only counts when you are moving about. In an ideal world I would own both - if only

money did grow on trees! For close up work I use three dedicated macro lenses. The 50mm, 100mm and 180mm macro lenses are all excellent but I must admit my favourite is the 100mm. It is usually the first out of the bag for static subjects and only if I need the specific view of either of the others will I change. I use 1.4x and very occasionally a 2x teleconverter when necessary as well as extension tubes of 12mm and 25mm at times.

Lighting and remote shooting

As much as possible I use natural light but when needed I will use flash. I have three 550EZ flash units, two Metz 45's and for high speed work I also use a set of three Fotronix high speed flash heads. These units were developed for photographers interested in capturing high speed action such as birds and bats in flight and overall they are very good. They are built superbly but do have some small faults with the flash bulbs themselves. I have used them successfully on a number of occasions and am happy to have them but they do have limitations.

With moving subjects it is often difficult get the composition you want using a remote triggering system. However, I will use remote systems for firing the camera if is the only way. I use the Canon LC3 infra red remote control to fire the camera if I can see the position of the camera and subject. However, for some subjects like birds flying from a window it would be impossible to fire the camera quickly enough to capture the image. In this case I use an infra red beam breaker system to fire the camera. I have been using one by a company called Phototrapper but during my work on the RTE television series 'Wild Trials' we found a system called 'The Time Machine' which is made by a company called Mumford electronics. It is a little more compact and therefore easier to use. Both these products are made in the USA and are only really needed if you are doing remote work on an ongoing basis.

Extras

Supporting the cameras during picture taking is extremely important for most of my work. My rule is simple - if I can use a tripod I will. Notable exceptions are when doing flight shots of birds which are not following the same flight path all the time or following butterflies and other insects around as they feed. I only use two tripods these days. The main one is the ultra heavy Gitzo 410 pro, which is very strong and stable and my first choice in most situations. It has no centre column which allows me to work very close to ground level, which is great for plants and also useful in some hide situations. If I need to walk long distances to a shooting position it is hard work bringing this tripod along due to its weight but always worth the effort in terms of stability in the end. I do have a lighter Manfrotto tripod which I will use if I am hiking a long distance and only using shorter focal length lenses. However when using the bigger lenses and especially the 600mm which weighs about 14lbs I will only use the heavier Gitzo. Some photographers are now choosing carbon fibre tripods as a way of reducing weight while still having a tripod with thick legs. I have never used one so can't really give an informed opinion on how good they are but it seems to me that the weight of a tripod will directly impact on its stability.

you would have to do with a ball and socket or pan and tilt head. The freedom this gives me, particularly when working in a hide is wonderful.

Field work

Some people hate working from hides yet most of the time I quite like it. The longest I've ever done in a hide is about 14 hours and I don't think I got the shot I wanted that day! The thing about working in a hide is that very often, if you are completely concealed, you get more than you bargained for. While waiting for a particular bird recently, a hare came past the front of the hide and was only about three metres away. This kind of thing regularly happens and it breaks the

I only use two tripod heads. For all lenses except the 600mm I use a Gitzo heavy duty ball and socket head which I find flexible enough for all situations. With the 600mm I use a Wimberley head which is a magical creation for big lenses. It is a gimbal type construction which allows a large heavy lens to appear almost weightless if mounted correctly and allows total freedom of movement in both the horizontal and vertical planes. It also allows the user to release their hold on the camera without having to screw it down as

monotony of waiting and you get some good shots of subjects you hadn't expected that day. If I can get away without using a hide I will but to get the close views I require of some of our more wary wildlife they are simply essential. I do have a commercially made hide from a company called Wildlife Watching Supplies but I often also use the elements around me to conceal myself. Some carefully placed scrim net hanging from an overhead branch can often be all that's needed. You can buy scrim netting from most hunting and fishing shops and its a cheap way to get started.

On a spring day during the making of the pictures for this book I had a small fox cub come so close to me when I was behind some scrim net that it was actually underneath the front of my 600mm lens!

For some subjects a hide is not a necessity. To photograph gulls at a pier, a bit of bread will usually do the trick and can get you some great images. Even small birds out in the garden or open countryside can often be photographed without a hide. The secret is often just to work slowly. If you rush towards a bird carrying a big tripod and camera the bird will usually fly off. If, on the other hand you watch from a distance for a while and find their favourite perches and then make a slow staggered approach, you will often get good results. Shooting from the car is also good at times. For some reason, birds which are wary of people on foot will often be quite happy if you park the car quite close to where they perch or feed. Open the window before you put the car in position and bring the camera over the window ledge slowly and you can get quite close views. Be careful where you park of course!

Baiting or "feeding in" of animals is something that has to be done at times. Providing it is done with sensitivity there is nothing wrong with it. We feed our garden birds artificially all the time and to me this is no different than making a feeding station for badgers or pine martens, everyone enjoys a free meal. Make sure you know what you are doing and that the food you are leaving out is not going to do the animals any harm. An example of this is that you regularly hear of people finding hedgehogs trapped in their garden netting and they feed them with bread and milk. They actually eat bugs, grubs, slugs and snails so something meaty like dog food is a much more appropriate meal.

Whether you are using a hide or not the best advice I can give is to know your subject. Learn about it. Watch it without a camera from a good distance and learn its habits and movements. Many subjects are quite habitual and will have established routines. A bird will often have a favourite perch, A fox may use the same track each time it goes out to hunt for food. An otter may fish at the same time of day at a certain place or at the same time of the tide in a coastal location. When you know what is going on it is easier to plan and be in the right place at the right time and use the light to your advantage.

Finally

Much of our wildlife is common and accessible to us for photography but you must have common sense and you must know the law. If a bird or animal is upset by your presence or actions, leave it alone immediately. For some subjects it is actually unlawful to photograph or disturb them at breeding times without a licence from the National Parks and Wildlife department. If in doubt, find out who your local Wildlife Ranger is and ask. Alternately go on to the government web site and print yourself a copy of the Wildlife Act. I work with rangers around the country all the time and they will usually be happy to help you out and let you know both the legality and common sense regarding photography of the wildlife around you. If you are a genuine photographer with good sense there is usually no problem in getting this assistance. However, there is loads of wildlife which is accessible to you in gardens, parks and local woodlands and this is a great place to start. A great image is a great image regardless of how common the subject matter. Be safe, respect your subjects and enjoy it.

Mike Brown

Special thanks to Pamela Anderson at Canon Consumer Imaging Ireland and Morgan Treacy at Pemberton Marketing for their assistance.

Further Reading

"A Place Near Heaven - A Year in West Cork"
By Damien Enright.
Published by Gill & McMacMillan.

"Complete Guide to Ireland's Birds - Second Edition"
By Eric Dempsey and Michael O'Clery.
Published by Gill & MacMillan.

"Ireland's Marine Life. A World of Beauty"
Editors Matt & Susan Murphy.
Photography: Paul Kay.
Published by Sherkin Island Marine Station.

"Ireland's Bird Life. A World of Beauty"
Editors Matt & Susan Murphy.
Photography: Richard Mills.
Published by Sherkin Island Marine Station.

"A Beginner's Guide to Ireland's Seashore"
Helena Challinor, Susan Murphy Wickens, Jane Clark, Audrey Murphy.
Photography: Paul Kay and Terry Farnell.
Published by Sherkin Island Marine Station.

"Nature in Ireland - A Scientific and Cultural History"
Edited by John Wilson Foster and Helena C.G. Chesney.
Published by Lilliput Press.

"Flora Hibernica – The Wild Flowers, Plants and Trees of Ireland"
By Jon Pilcher and Valerie Hall.
Published by Collins Press.

"Kerry A Natural History"
By Terry Carruthers.
Collins Press.

"Wild Plants of the Burren and Aran Islands"
By Charles E. Nelson.
Published by Collins Press.

"A Place to Treasure: Killarney National Park"
Edited by Bill Quirke.
Published by Collins Press.

"Ireland - A Smithsonian Natural History"
By Micahel Viney.
Published by Blackstaff Press.

"The Way That I Went. An Irishman in Ireland"
New Introduction by Michael Viney. By Robert Lloyd Praeger.
Published by Collins Press.

"Ireland's Wild Countryside"
By Éamon de Buitléar.
Published by Boxtree Limited.

"The Animals of Ireland"
By Gordon D'Arcy.
Published by Appletree Press Ltd.

"Birds of Ireland"
By Gordon D'Arcy.
Published by Appletree Press Ltd.

"Wildlife"
By Don Conroy and Chris Wilson.
Published by Mentor Press.

"Wildlife Quiz and Amazing Facts Book"
By Don Conroy and Chris Wilson.
Published by Natural Rapture Ltd.

"Wild and Wonderful"
By Éanna Ní Lamhna.
Published by Townhouse.